from the Archives

OF THE UNIVERSE CATHOLIC WEEKLY

Volume Three

A Universe special publication

Photographs continue to reveal our rich heritage

Welcome to the third volume of photographs from *The Universe* archives project – an initiative that is preserving and restoring the newspaper's unique collection of more than 20,000 photographs and illustrations depicting Catholic life, from the founding of the paper in 1860, to the present day.

In many respects the history of *The Universe* Catholic weekly photo collection mirrors the development of photojournalism itself. Founded only a decade after the restoration of the hierarchy in England, *The Universe* was one of the first newspapers to make regular use of photography as it sought to convey to its readers the progress of public Catholicism in these islands. Many of the great events of the closing years of the 19th and opening years of the 20th centuries were essentially private affairs where – depute their significance – press access was extremely limited. The photographers at *The Universe* were therefore in a unique position to record these events, and to circulate their pictures for wider press use.

Throughout the last century the newspaper passed through many hands, and saw its premises moved numerous times. Remarkably, its unique collection of glass slides and negatives survived right up to the 1970s, when a move from London to Manchester brought with it the catastrophic decision to scrap the collection – partly for economy of space, but mainly because thinking at the time put no significant value on preserving the past. (It was during these years, for instance, that the BBC and ITV destroyed countless unique recordings of early, classic television series whose loss is greatly regretted today.)

By sheer luck, the best of the *Universe* negatives had been made into prints for consideration by the newsdesk and, thanks to the diligence of a succession of clerical assistants, these pictures, whether used or not, were meticulously marked and filed for possible future use. Stored alongside the newspaper's general library files, these unique prints were transferred to Manchester in the late70s, but fell into disuse as the collection became outdated, and electronic imaging became more commonplace.

They survived a further attempt to scrap them in the early 90s, after which they lay dormant in their filing cabinets at the back of our library until 2003, when I began the task of archiving them electronically. It was a desperately urgent job, as the extremely dry conditions had caused many of the prints to become brittle, and the photographic emulsion was cracking and separating the images from their backing paper. Just taking the images out into the daylight was also perilous, as most had been producing in quick fixing chemicals designed for strictly short term efficiency, and were no longer light tolerant.

Three years into the project the prints themselves have been stabilised, and the work of scanning the images and recording information goes on. Thanks to a separate project of restoring and preserving our bound editions of *The Universe*, I have also begun to cross-reference the images to the relevant edition of the newspaper, which has added greatly to their informational value. After the previous two volumes of *From The Archives*, many of you asked if more information could be provided with the images in this volume, and I've tried to do this wherever possible. Unfortunately many of the photographs, whilst fascinating to look at, contain little information beyond a caption or brief news story. Some, however, have yielded fascinating and otherwise unrecorded stories of Catholic life and endeavour.

I hope you enjoy this latest sample of highlights from the project, and that they will help to enrich your appreciation of our great and significant Catholic heritage.

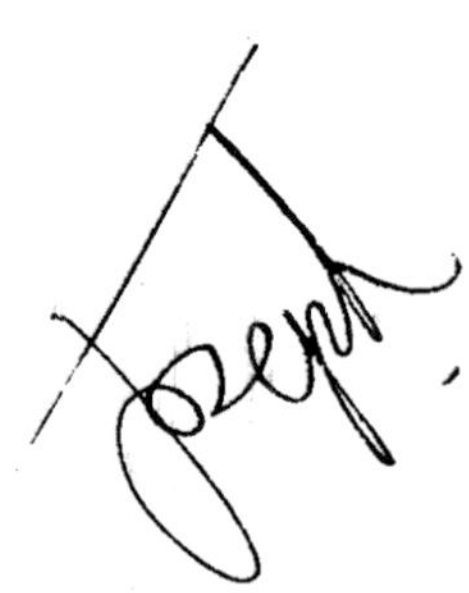

Joseph Kelly

Editorial Director:
Gabriel Communications Ltd

Editor:
The Universe
Who's Who in Catholic Life
From The Archives

Front cover: They remember the Catholic martyrs: part of a procession of more than 1,000 people who marched from Newgate to Tyburn, on the 1961 Annual Tyburn walk. The walk, organised by the Guild of our Lady of Ransom, commemorated over 100 Catholic martyrs who were hanged, drawn and quartered in the 16th and 17th centuries. They were dragged on hurdles from Newgate Prison (now the Old Bailey) to their death at Tyburn gallows (where Marble Arch stands today).

Right: A crowd gathers in London's Soho Square, during the April 1967 Tyburn Walk.

Back cover: Irish President Mary Robinson greets Cardinal Basil Hume as John Major looks on in Downing Street on 5th June 1996. Mrs. Robinson was on a four-day visit to Britain.

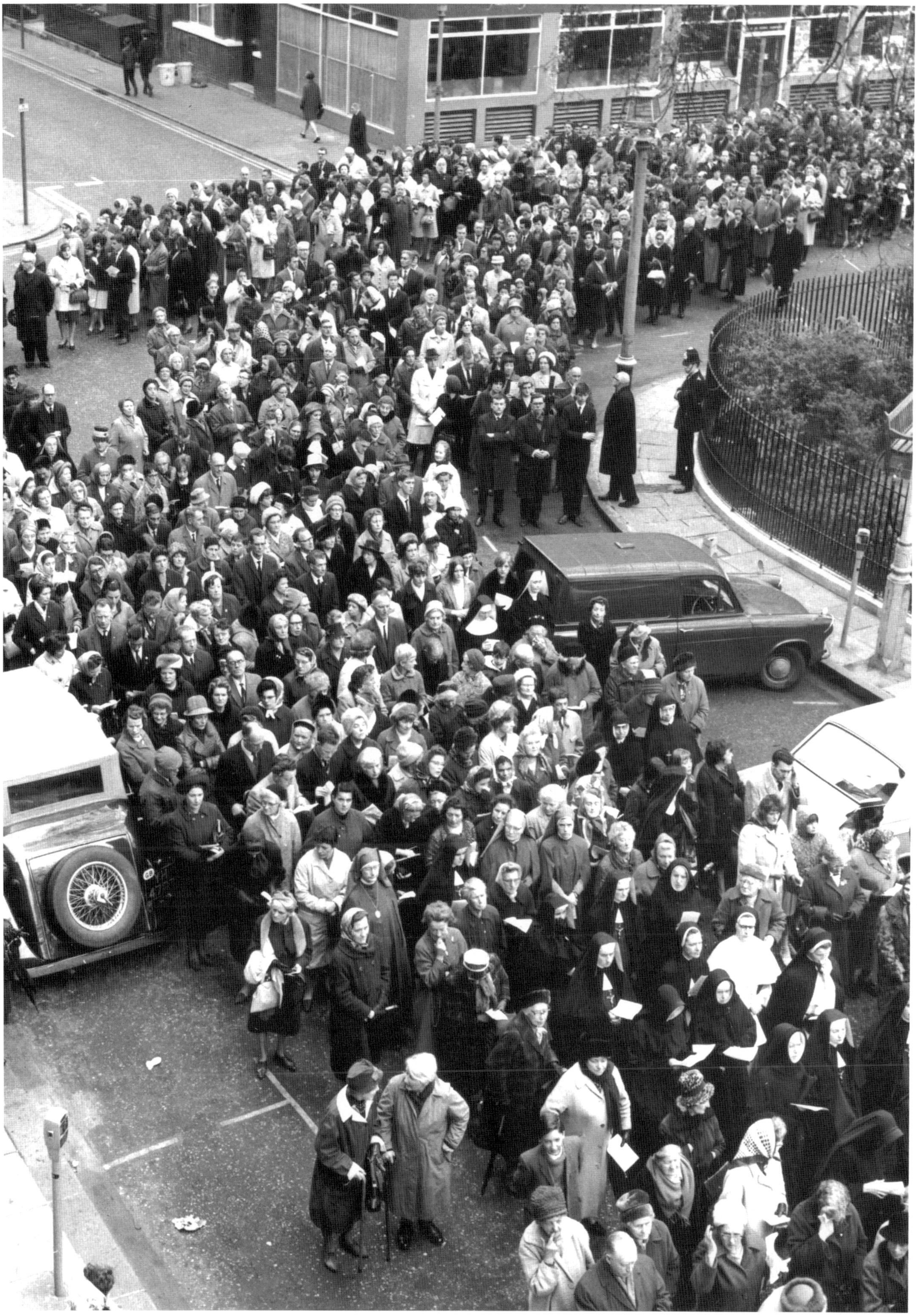

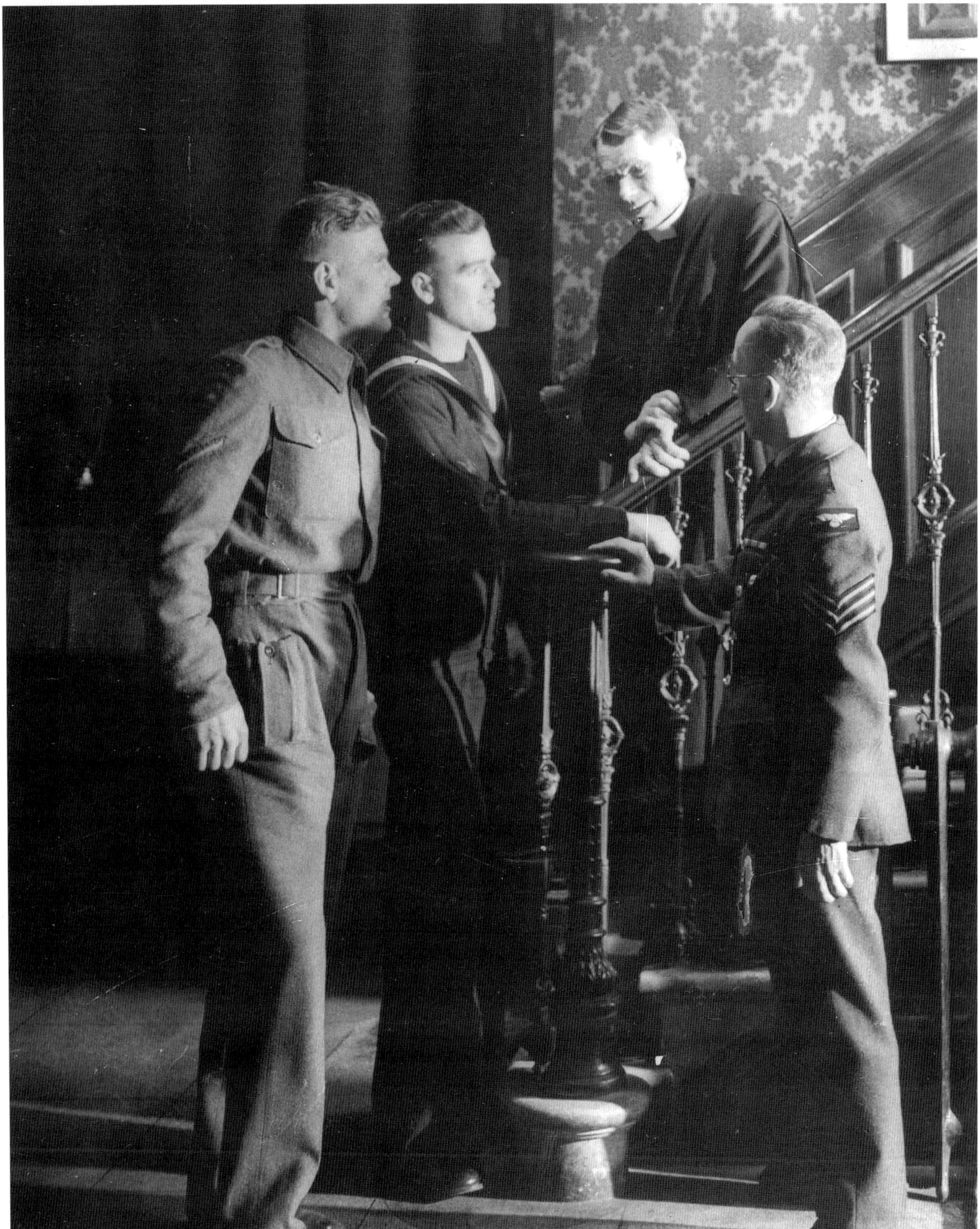

Preparing themselves for the ordeal of invasion, men of the Allied Forces discuss their spiritual problems with Fr. Clement Tigar SJ, during a weekend retreat at Campion House, Osterley, Middlesex, in April 1944. Thirty years later, on 4th October 1974, *The Universe* reported that Fr. Tigar was "celebrating the golden jubilee of his ordination quietly by offering Mass at St. Mary's, Ryde, Isle of Wight". Fr. Tigar was appointed to succeed Campion House's founder, Fr, Edmund Lester, in 1935. In his 31 years at Osterley he saw 637 of his former pupils ordained, 16 per cent of all priests in England and Wales at the time. During the war he held regular retreats for the troops at Campion House. Some of his retreatants even returned from the war to study for the priesthood. He is pictured above with troops on retreat just before the D-Day invasion of France. Fr. Tigar was also widely known for his devotion to the Forty Martyrs and was for many years the leading advocate of their canonisation cause, and wrote an influential book on the subject.

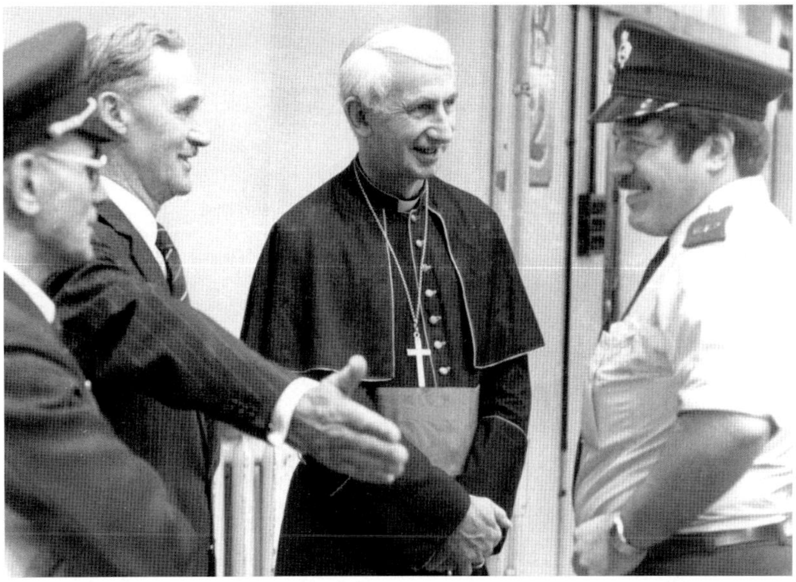

"I love visiting prisons," Cardinal Hume said following a two and a half hour visit to Pentonville in September 1977. The cardinal is pictured being introduced to staff by the Governor, Mr. Roland Adams.

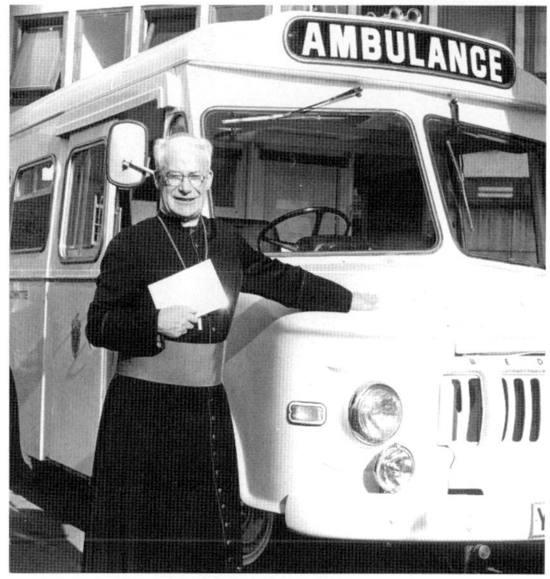

Bishop Holland of Salford dedicating a new coronary care ambulance after it had been presented to Hope Hospital, Salford in October 1972.

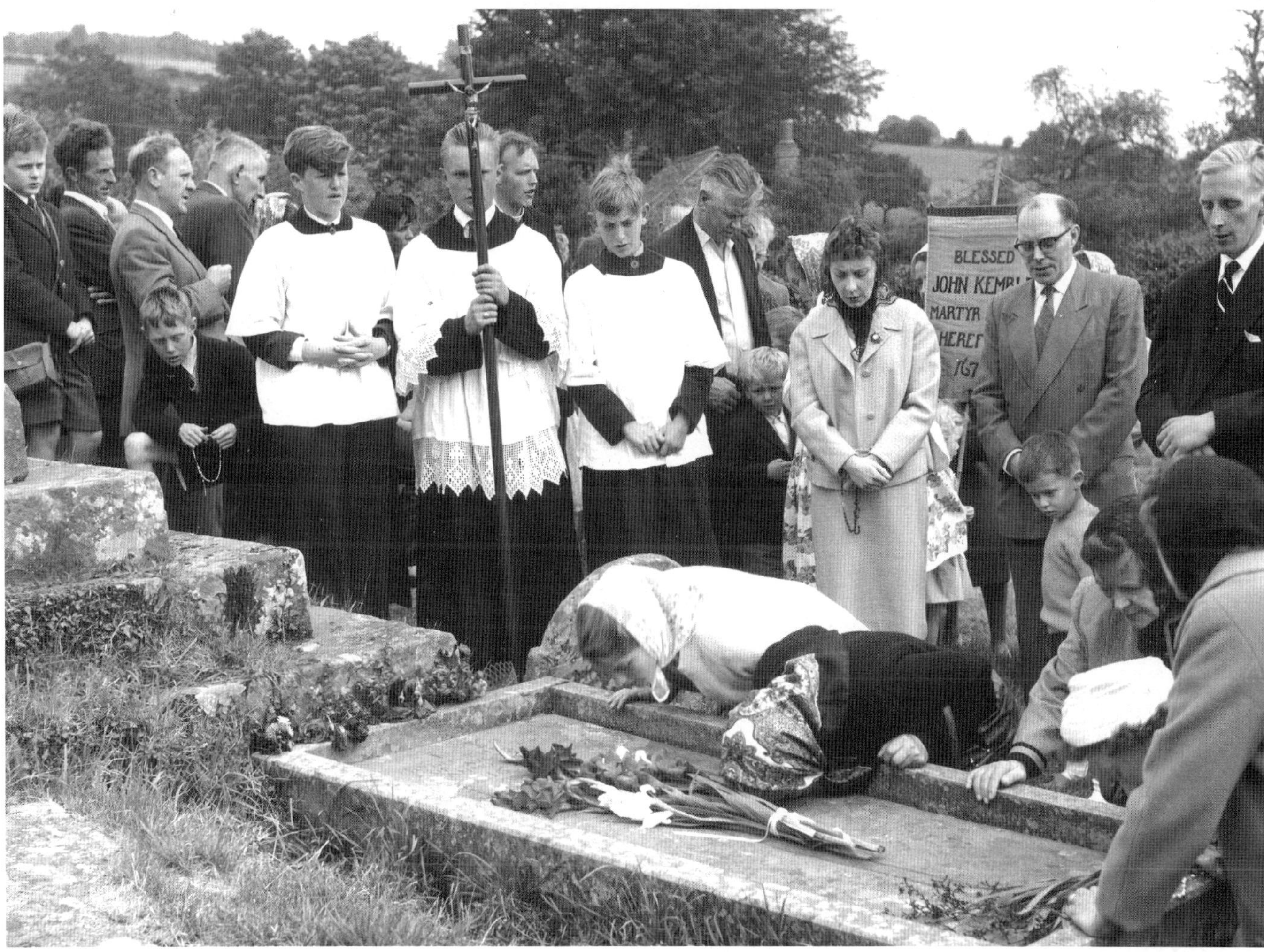

Pilgrims kneel and kiss the grave of Blessed (later saint) John Kemble, at Welsh Newtown in August 1961. John Kemble was born at Rhydicar Farm, St. Weonard's, Herefordshire, in 1599, into a prominent local Catholic family which boasted four other priests. He was ordained a priest at Douai College, France, on 23rd February 1625, and returned to England on 4th June 1625 as a missioner in Monmouthshire and Herefordshire. Little is known of his work caring for the sustenance of his flock for the next 53 years. The conditions for Catholics had eased from the ferocious persecution of the Elizabethan period, but the priest performed his ministry discreetly. What we can deduce from his later treatment was the esteem and affection he was held in locally. He was falsly implicated in the Titus Oates plot of 1678. The then 80 year old priest was sentenced to be hung, drawn and quartered at Hereford, but it was agreed, because of his frailty, to allow him to die before disembowelling and quartering of his body took place. The execution took place at Widemarsh Common, Hereford, on 22nd August, 1679, but the executioner so botched his task that the ageing Fr. Kemble hung on the gallows for more than half an hour before being declared dead. One of his hands is preserved at St. Francis Xavier, Hereford, and his body lies in the (C of E) churchyard of St. Mary's, Welsh Newtown, near Hereford, to which Catholics still make an annual pilgrimage.

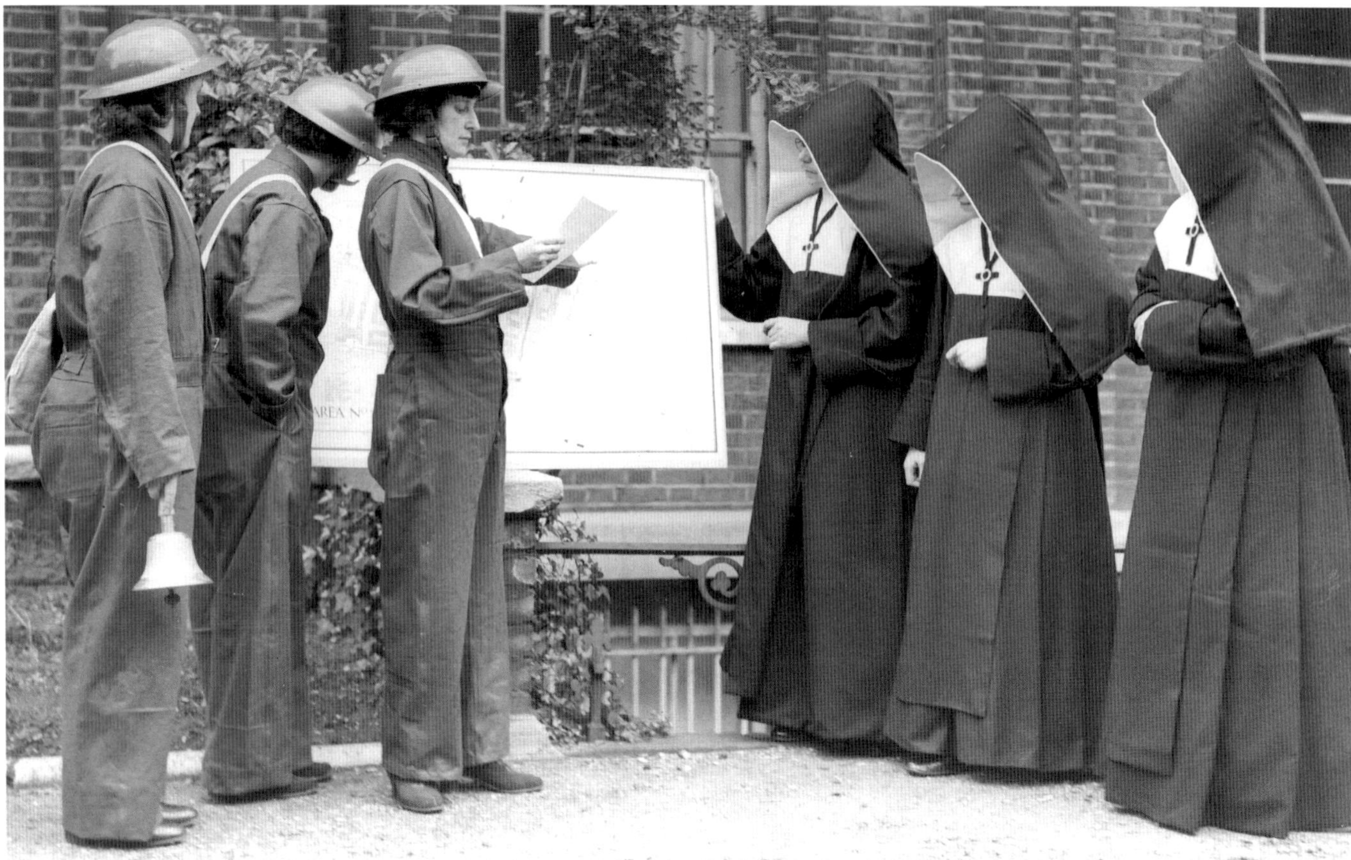

Daughters of the Cross of St. Wilfred's Convent, Chelsea, took part in the 'great daylight ARP test' which took place in London in June 1939. The *Universe* photographer caught this group receiving their final instructions from wardens.

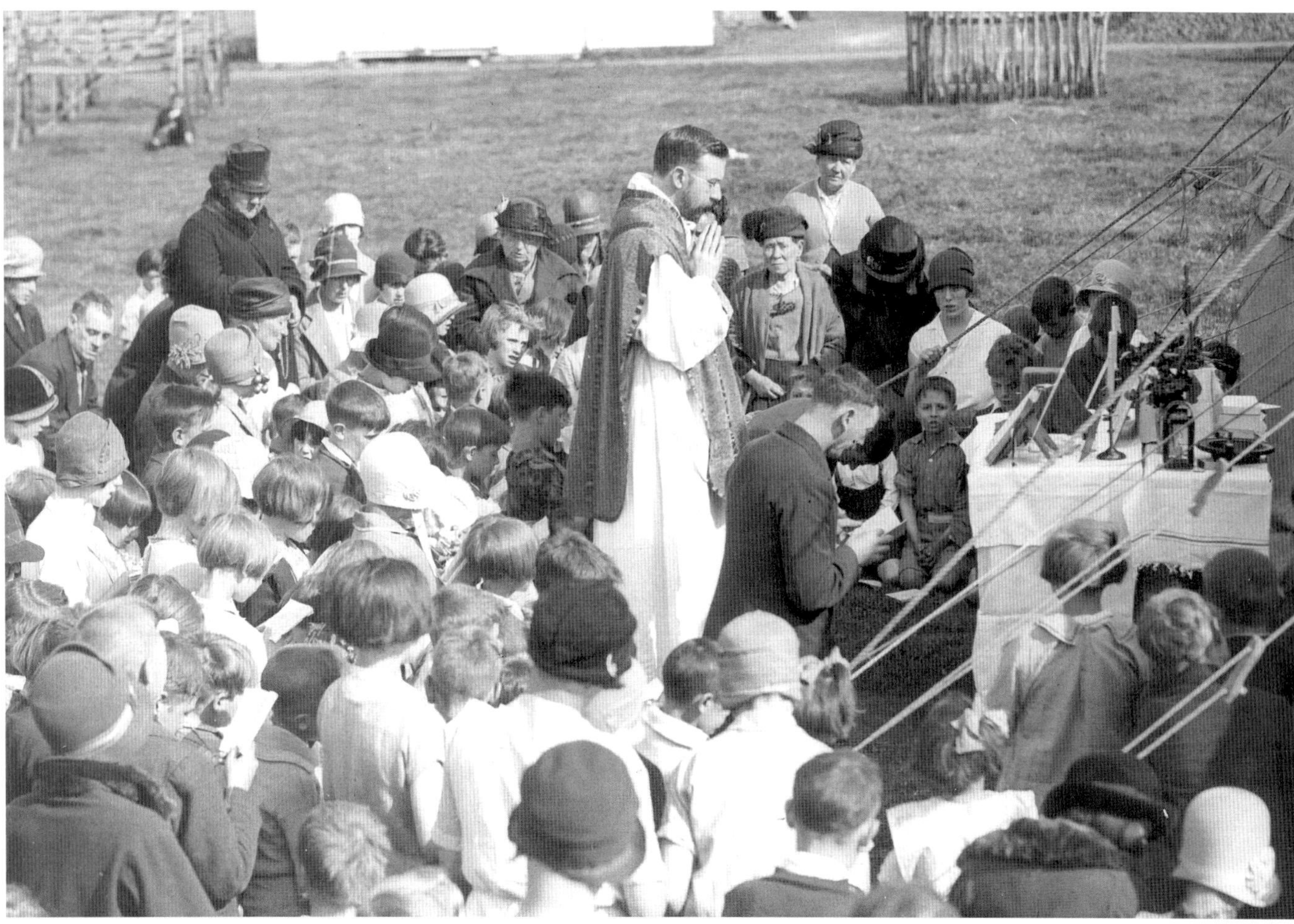

Open air Mass at a makeshift altar for hop pickers in the fields of Kent, in September 1923. The Franciscan Fathers had established temporary mission centres in various parts of the hopfields, and were assisted by members of the Catholic Women's League.

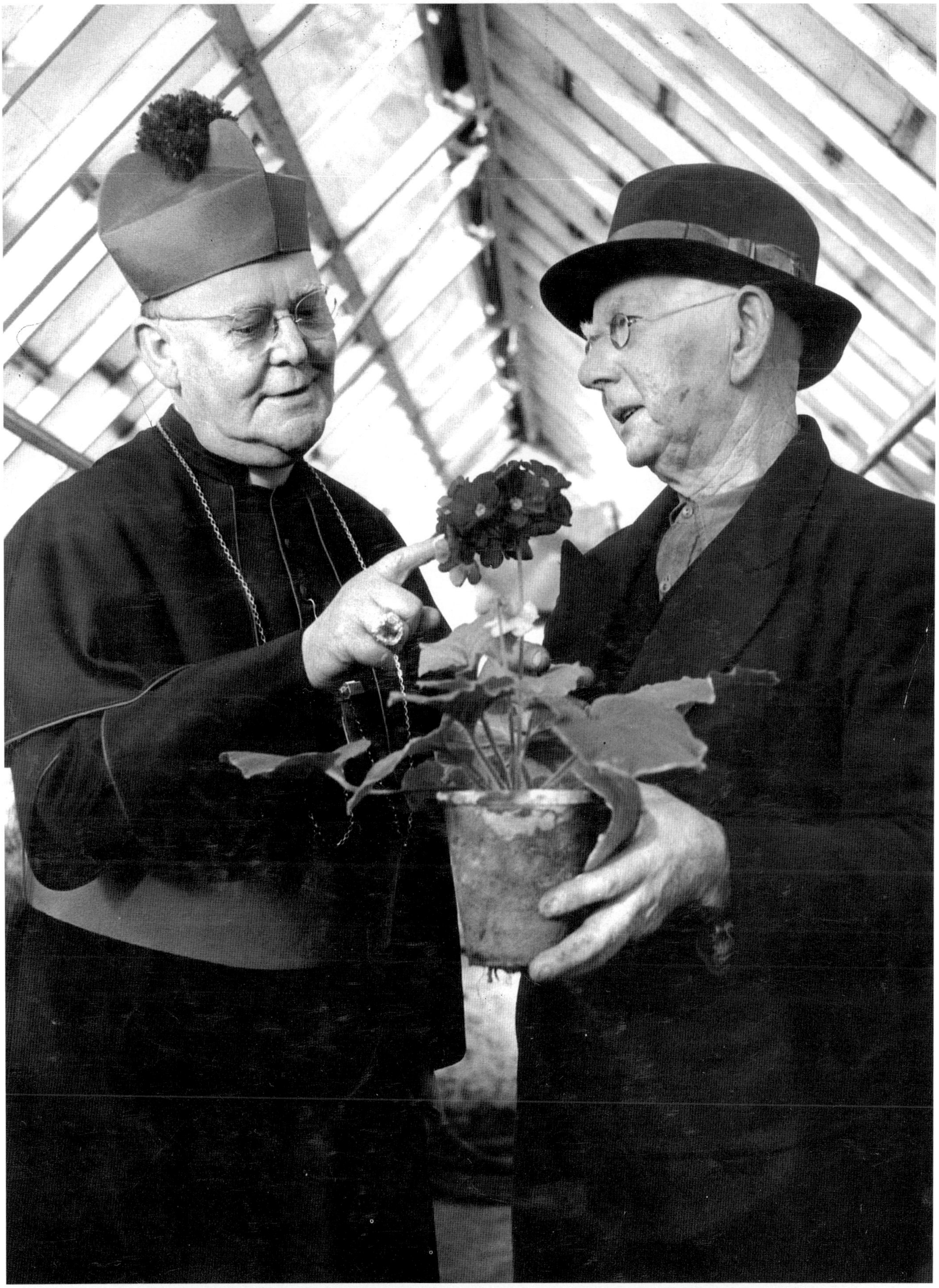

The newly appointed Archbishop of Westminster, Monsignor Godfrey, says goodbye to his favourite flowers before travelling from Liverpool to London for his enthronement on 11th February 1957. Mgr. Godfrey told *The Universe* that one of his regrets at leaving Liverpool was that "he will say goodbye to John Rigg, his faithful gardener, and to his potted plants which he inspects daily." He is pictured making one of his last visits to the greenhouse into which he called after morning prayers in his private chapel on most days during his time in office at Liverpool.

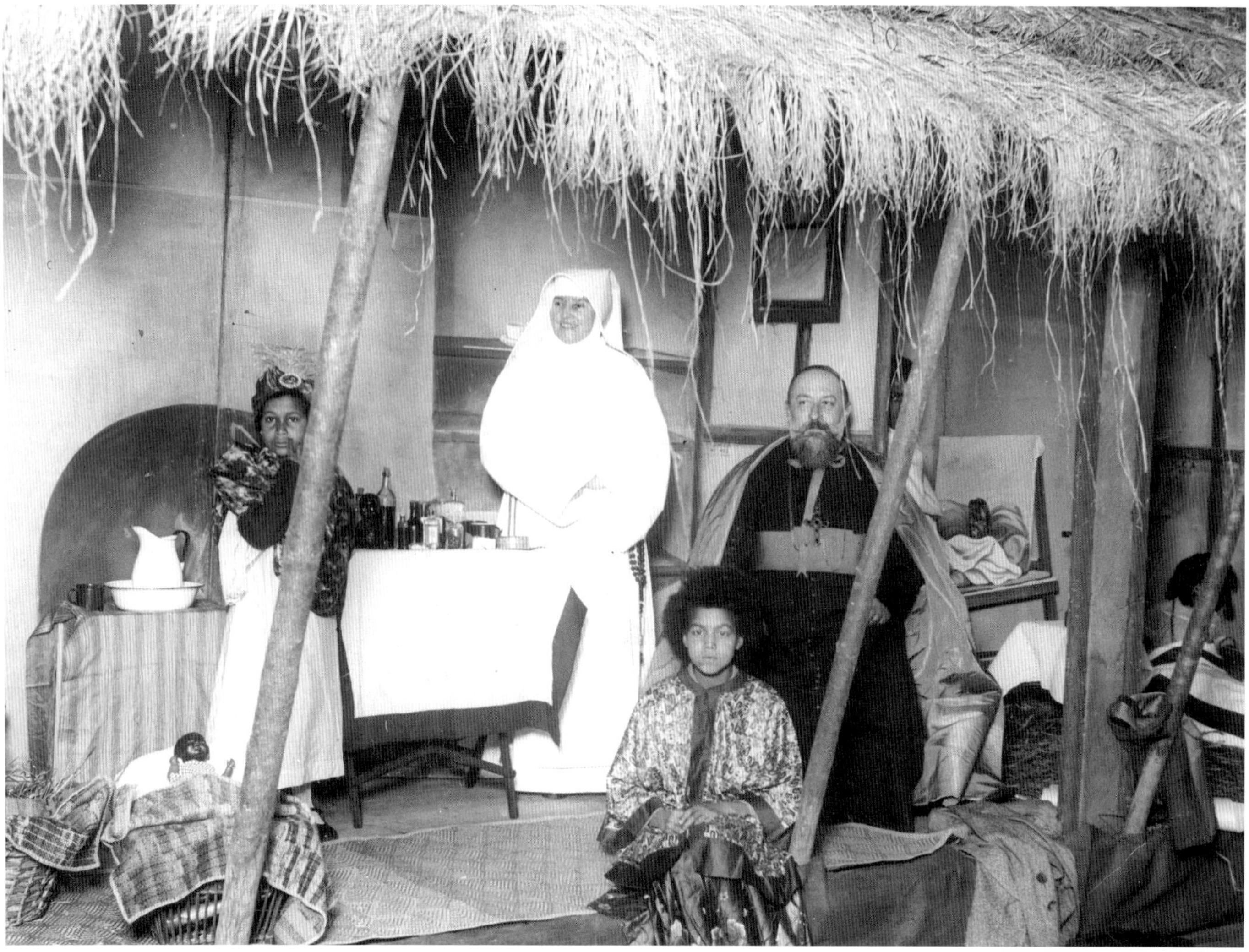

Remarkably, this photograph was not taken in a remote mission station, but at Cathedral Hall, Westminster in November 1929. Pictured are Bishop Johannes Biermans MHM, Vicar Apostolic Emeritus of Upper Nile and Titular Bishop of Gargara and his assistant Mother Kevin, who agreed to man this recreation of a 'native dispensary' which formed part of a model of an African village erected in the hall for a missionary exhibition. Bishop Biermans, a pioneer missionary who had been working in Uganda, was elected Superior General of the Mill Hill missionaries in 1924.

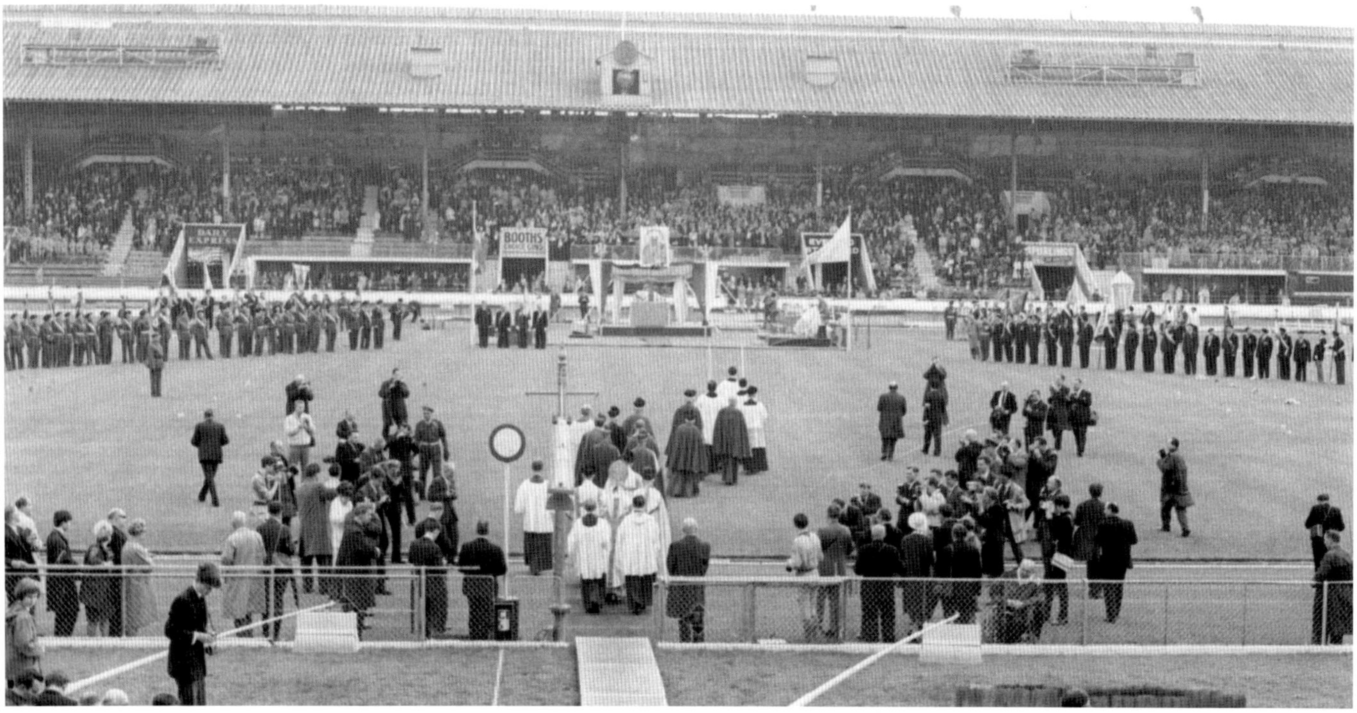

The *Universe* photographer was on hand to capture this panorama at the White City stadium in London on 22 May 1966, during Polish Millennium celebrations, marking 1,000 years of the Catholic faith in their country.

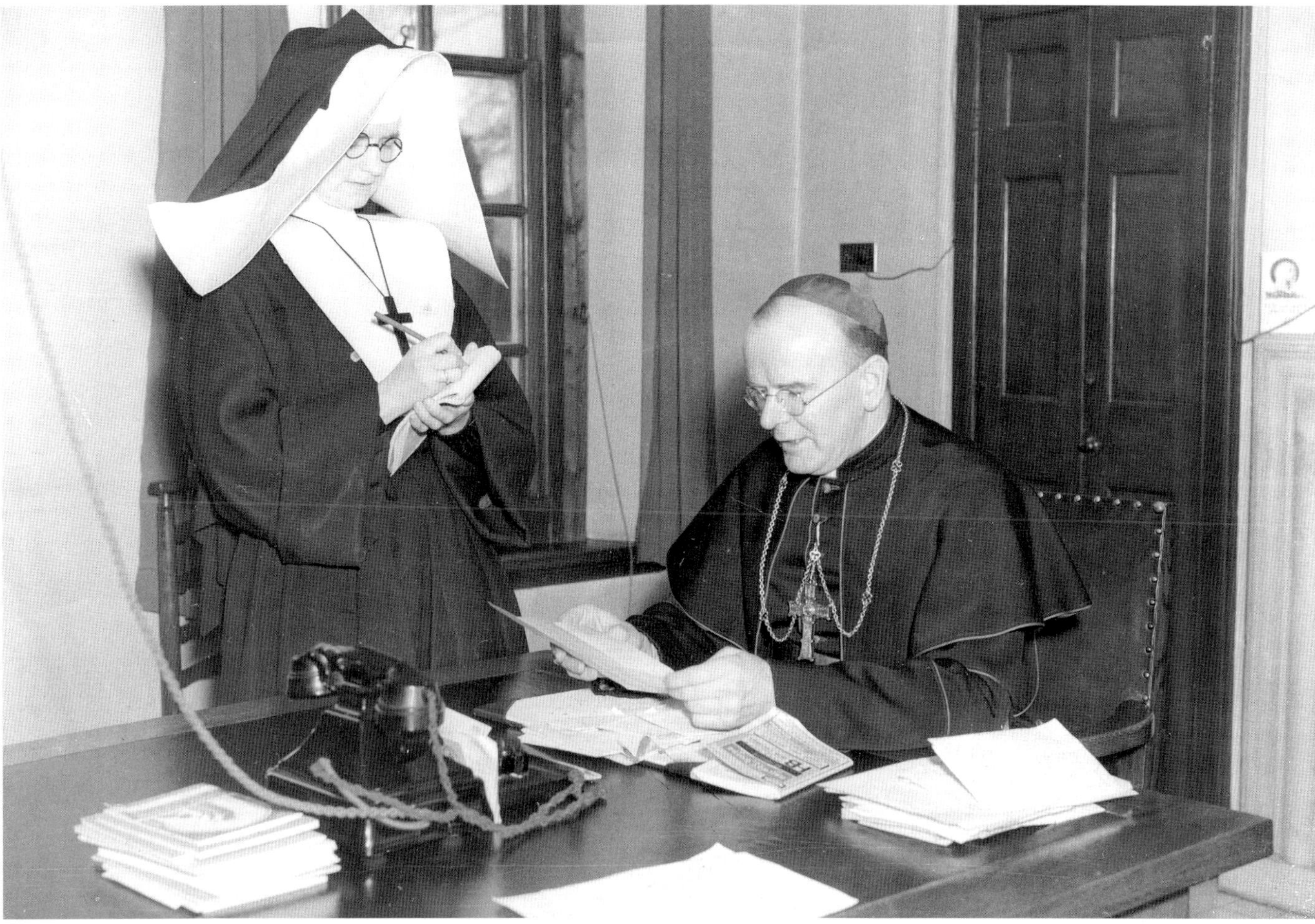

Business of the day starts at 9am for Dr. Bernard Griffin, as he dictates correspondence to one of his secretaries, Sr. M. Adrienne in 1943 shortly after being appointed Archbishop of Westminster. Born in Birmingham, on 21st February 1899, he was educated at Cotton College, Oscott, the Venerable English College and the Beda. He was ordained in 1924 and three years later became Secretary for 10 years to the Archbishop of Birmingham. He was Chancellor of the Diocese at 30 and a notable Administrator of its charitable homes. In 1938 he was made Auxiliary Bishop of Birmingham and during the war period succeeded Cardinal Hinsley as Archbishop of Westminster in 1943. Three years later, at the age of 47, he was created Cardinal. His links with social welfare helped him deal with the new post-war Labour Government as it carried out sweeping and widespread social reforms. He journeyed frequently abroad on Church affairs until stricken by illness which hampered his last years. He died on the 20 August 1956, at the age of 57.

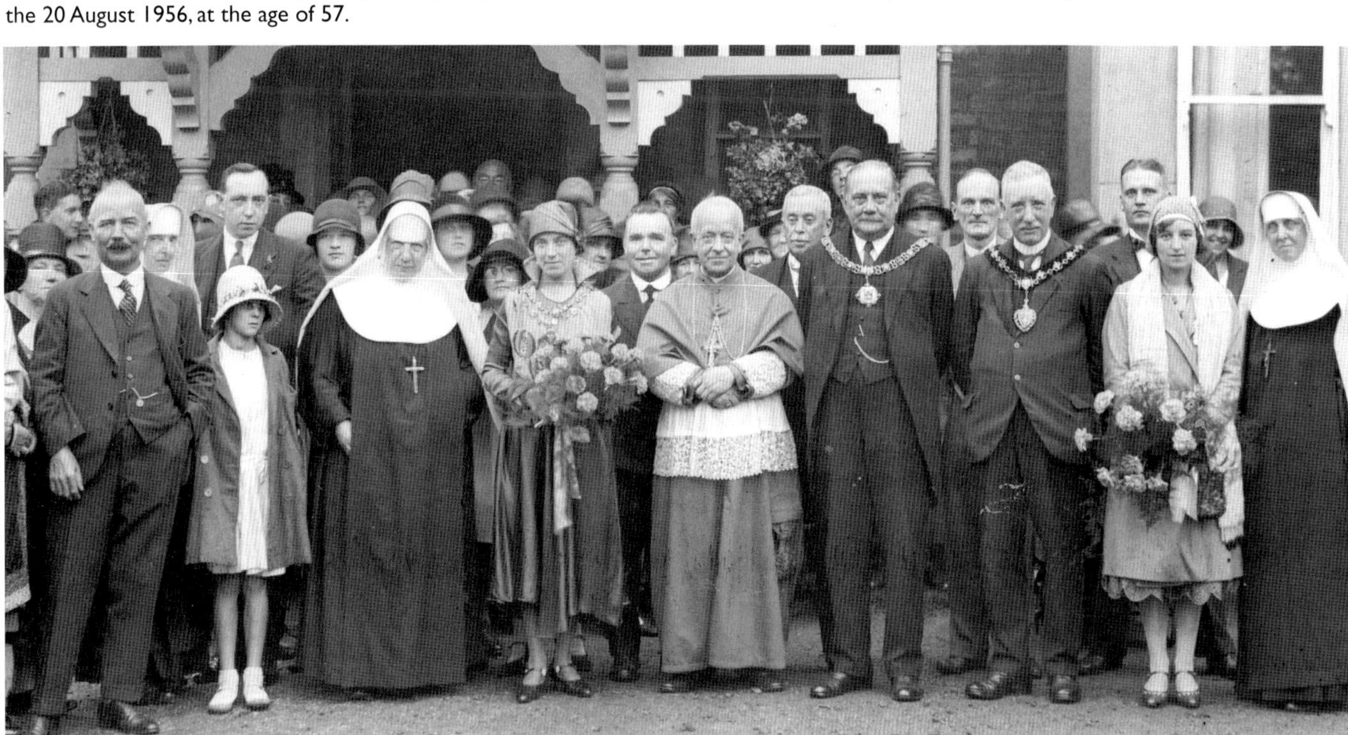

A group at the opening and blessing by the Bishop of Nottingham of the new nursing home for the 'Blue Nuns' at Weedthorpe, Nottingham in September 1930. Included in the group are the Lord Mayor and Mayoress and the Sheriff of Nottingham.

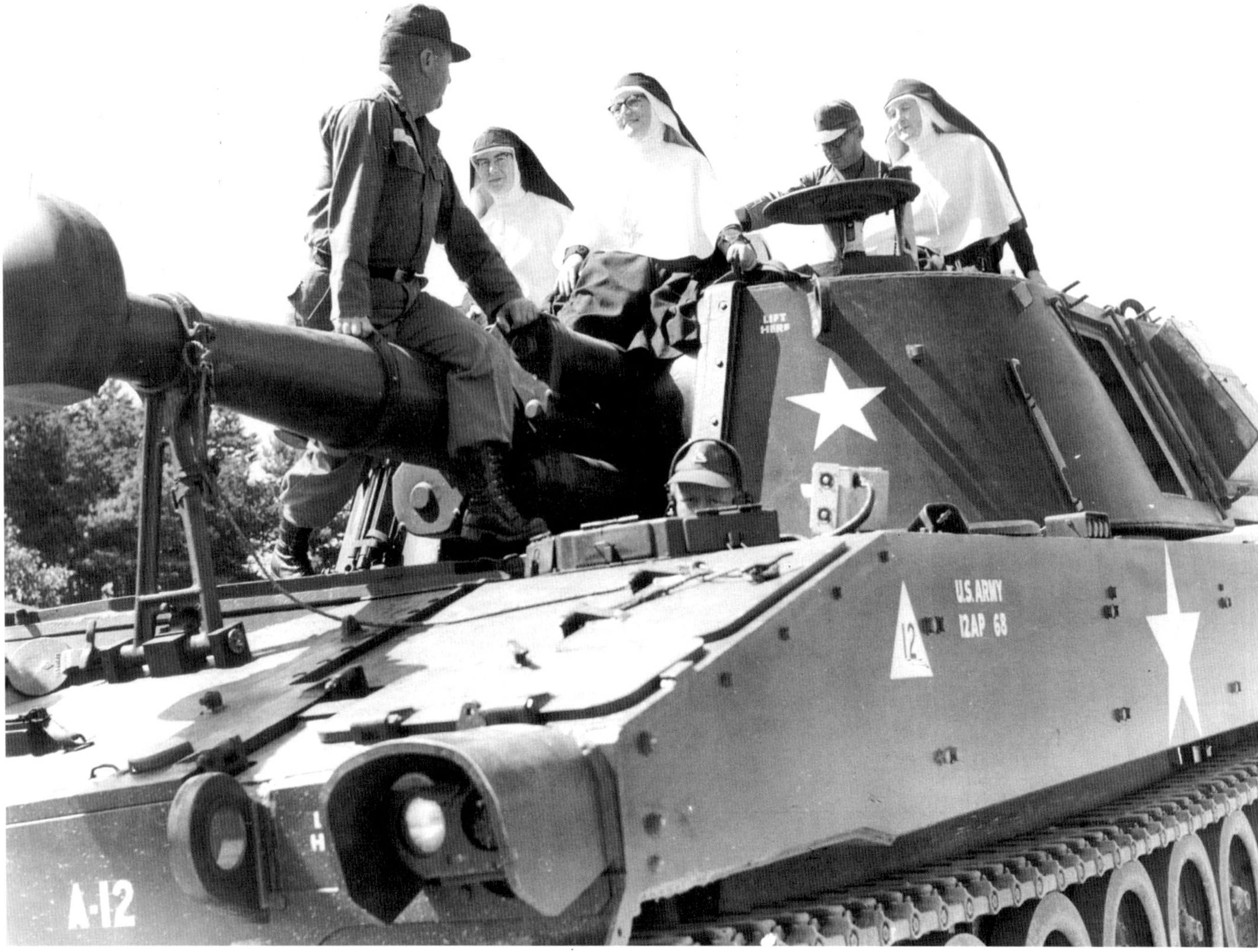

Marist nuns from England try their hand at tank driving during a break in a visit to Germany in October 1965. The nuns made an annual trip to do catechetical work among the children of members of the U.S. Forces based in the Rhineland.

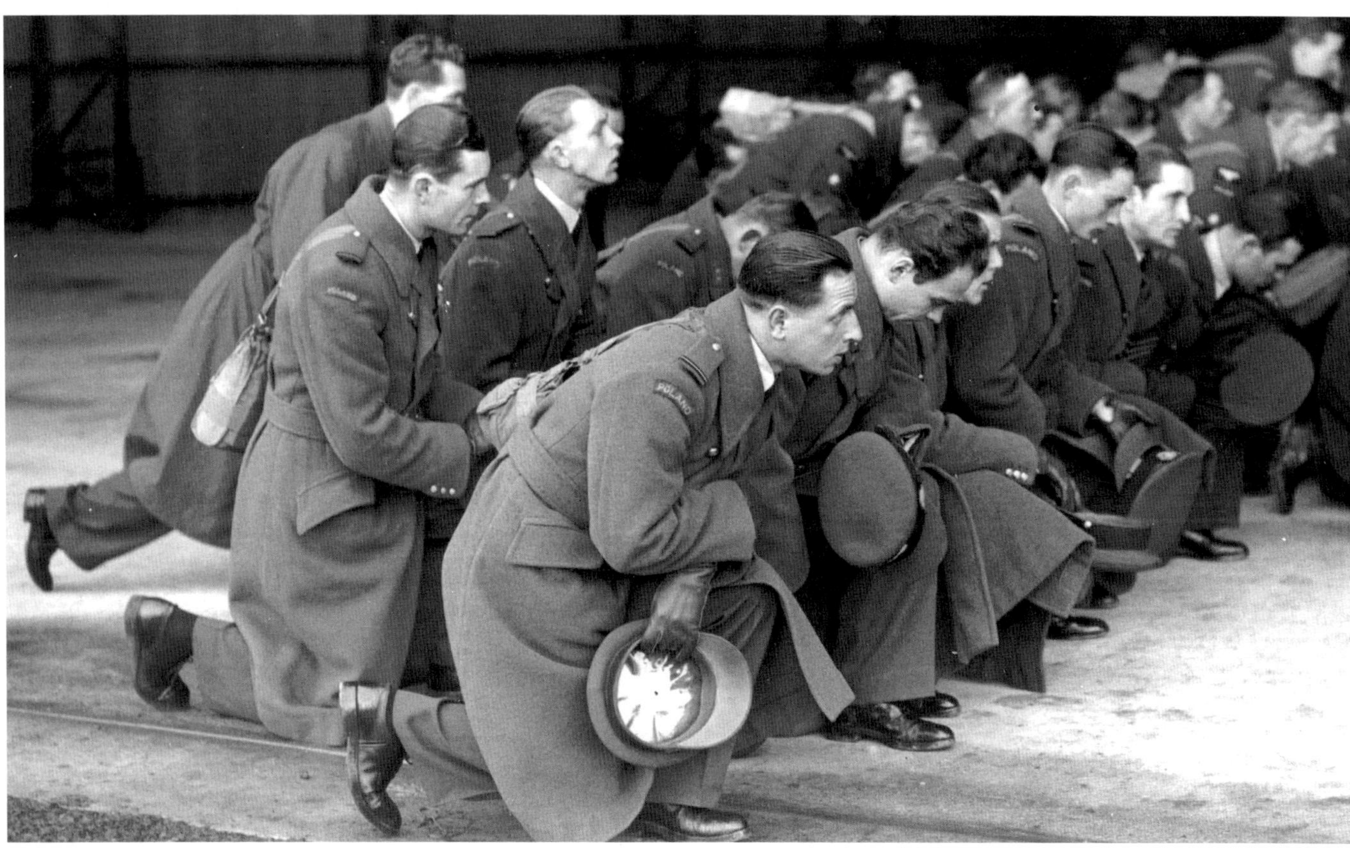

Polish pilots kneel in a hangar "somewhere in England" during Mass, celebrated by their Polish chaplain in November 1941.

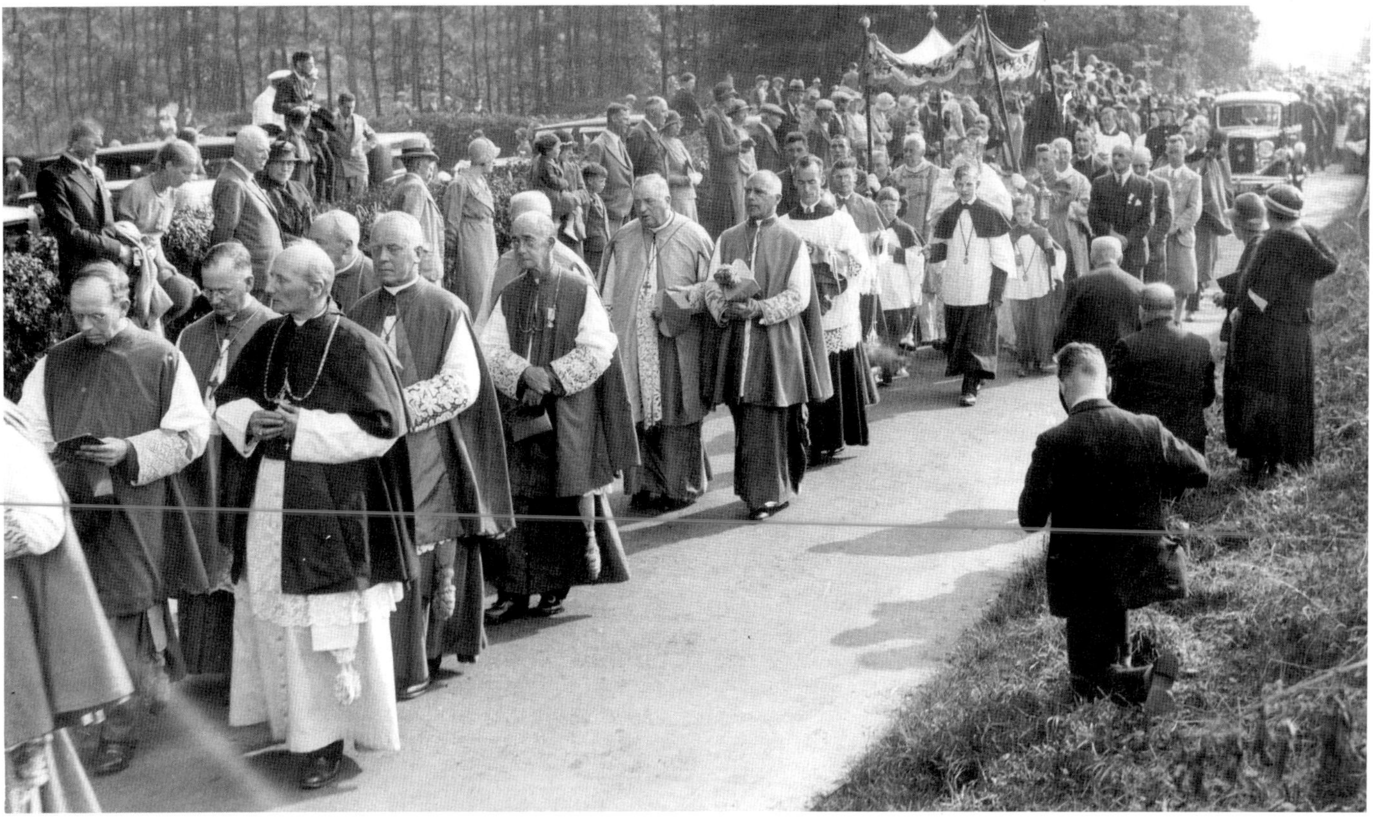

A remarkable moment in English Catholic history, captured by a *Universe* photographer on 19th August 1934. Cardinal Bourne (riding in car) and the English bishops lead 3,000 pilgrims in procession to honour Our Lady of Walsingham, at Walsingham, Norfolk, in the first Catholic procession in this holy spot since the Reformation. A request to Lady Gurney, who owned the grounds, for permission for the pilgrimage to enter the priory grounds, was refused, according the *Universe* report of the event. The pilgrims attended Pontifical High Mass in the church of St. John the Baptist at Norwich, and afterwards went to the Slipper Chapel where an open air altar had been built on the banks of the Stiffkey. The Sacrament was carried by the Bishop of Northampton.

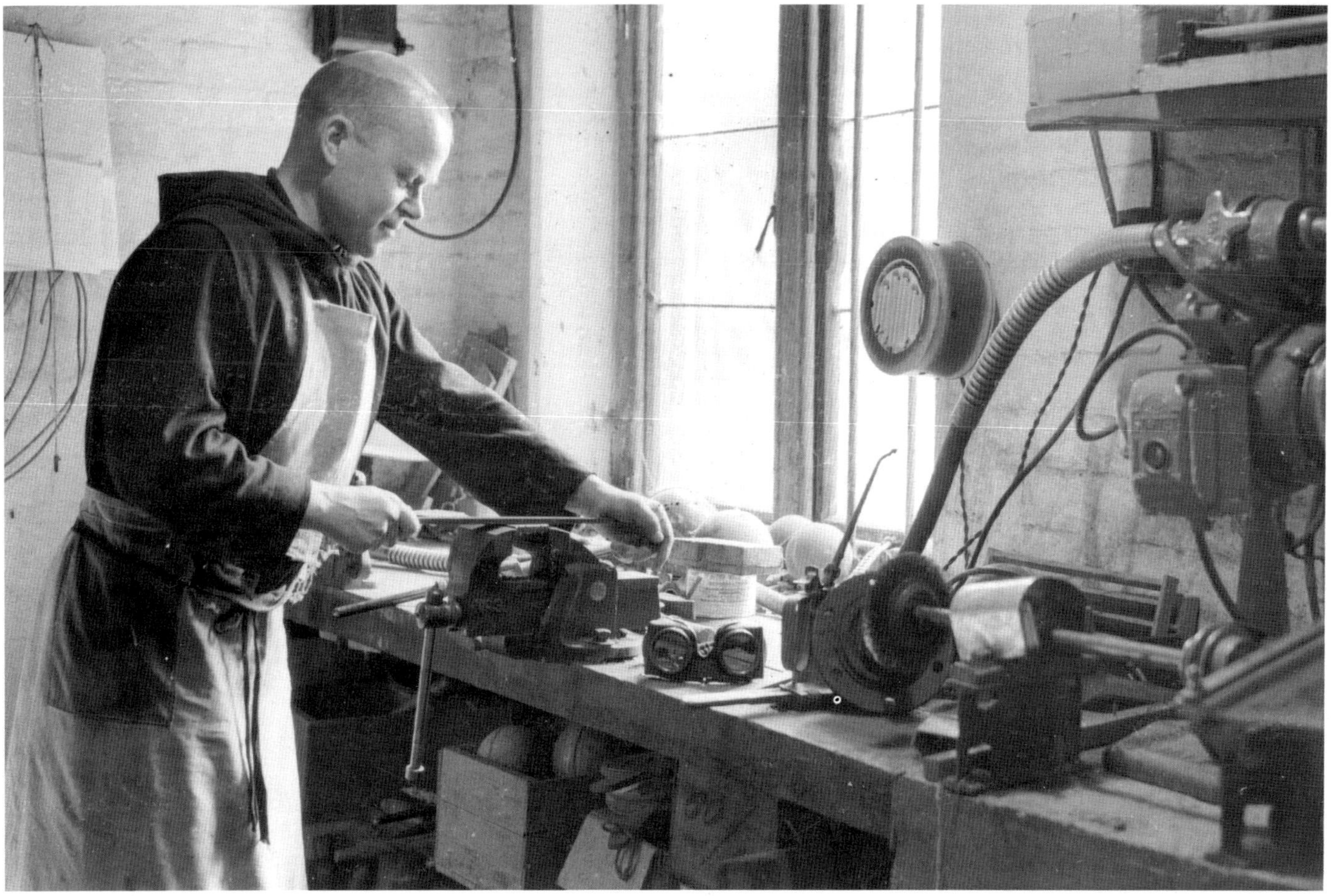

In the workshop at Quarr Abbey a monk is pictured at the engineer's bench in November 1954, using what the *Universe* described as "modern electrical lathes and oxy-acetylene burners" for welding.

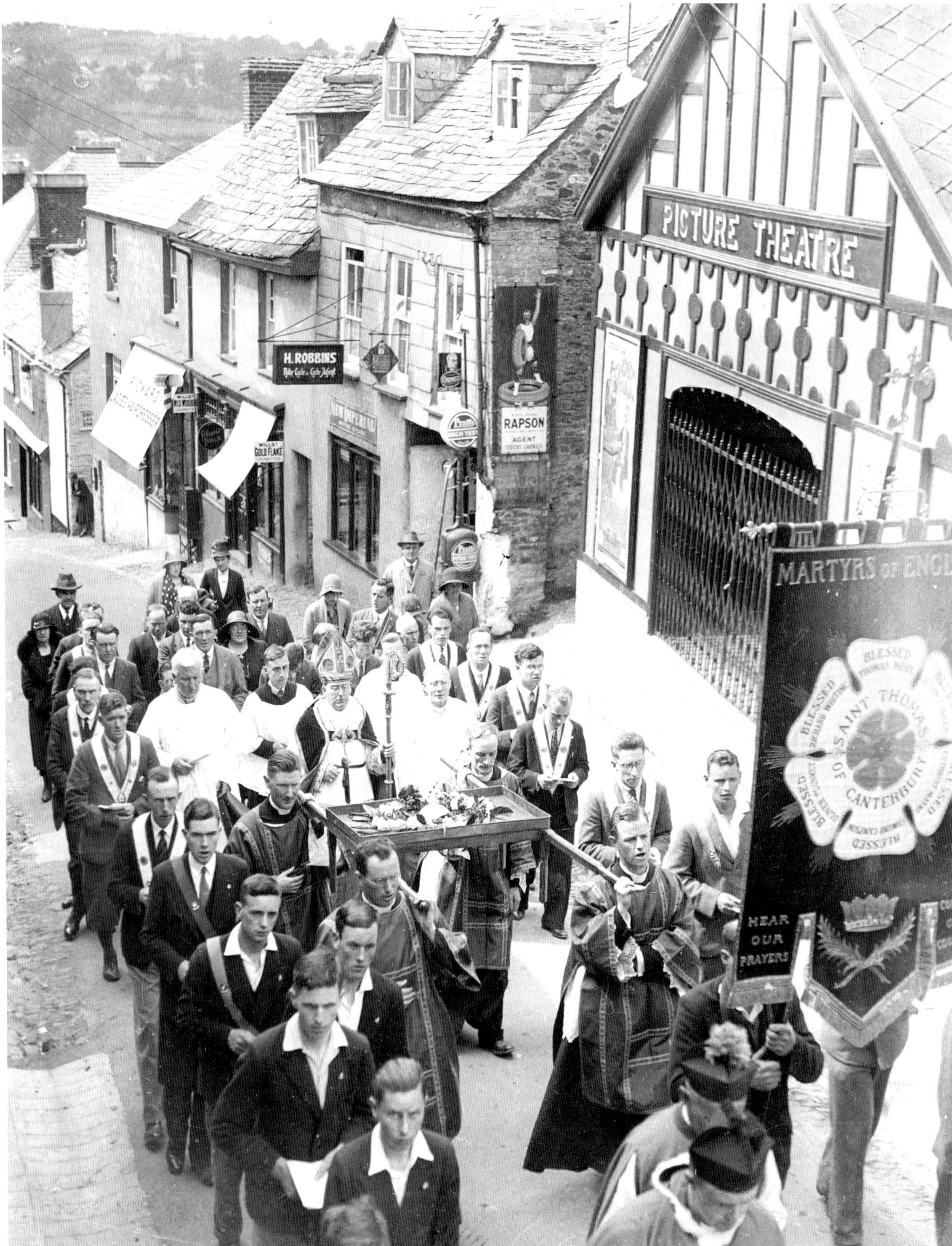

Bishop Barrett follows the relics of Blessed Cuthbert Mayne in a pilgrimage in the martyr's honour at Launceston, Cornwall, on Sunday 17 June 1932. Bishop John Patrick Barrett was born in Liverpool in 1878 and became Auxiliary Bishop of Birmingham in 1926. He was appointed Bishop of Plymouth diocese on the 7th June 1929, and he died on the 2nd November 1946. St Cuthbert Mayne was a convert to the Catholic faith who was martyred in horrific fashion in 1577. He was canonised by Pope Paul VI in 1970. Visitors to St. Cuthbert Mayne RC church, St. Stephen's Hill, Launceston, can see his shrine, which includes a relic of the saint's skull and the "Inspeximus" issued by the Crown to Sir George Carey in 1581, giving details of the charge against Cuthbert Mayne. The latter provides evidence that the saint suffered martyrdom solely because of his religion.

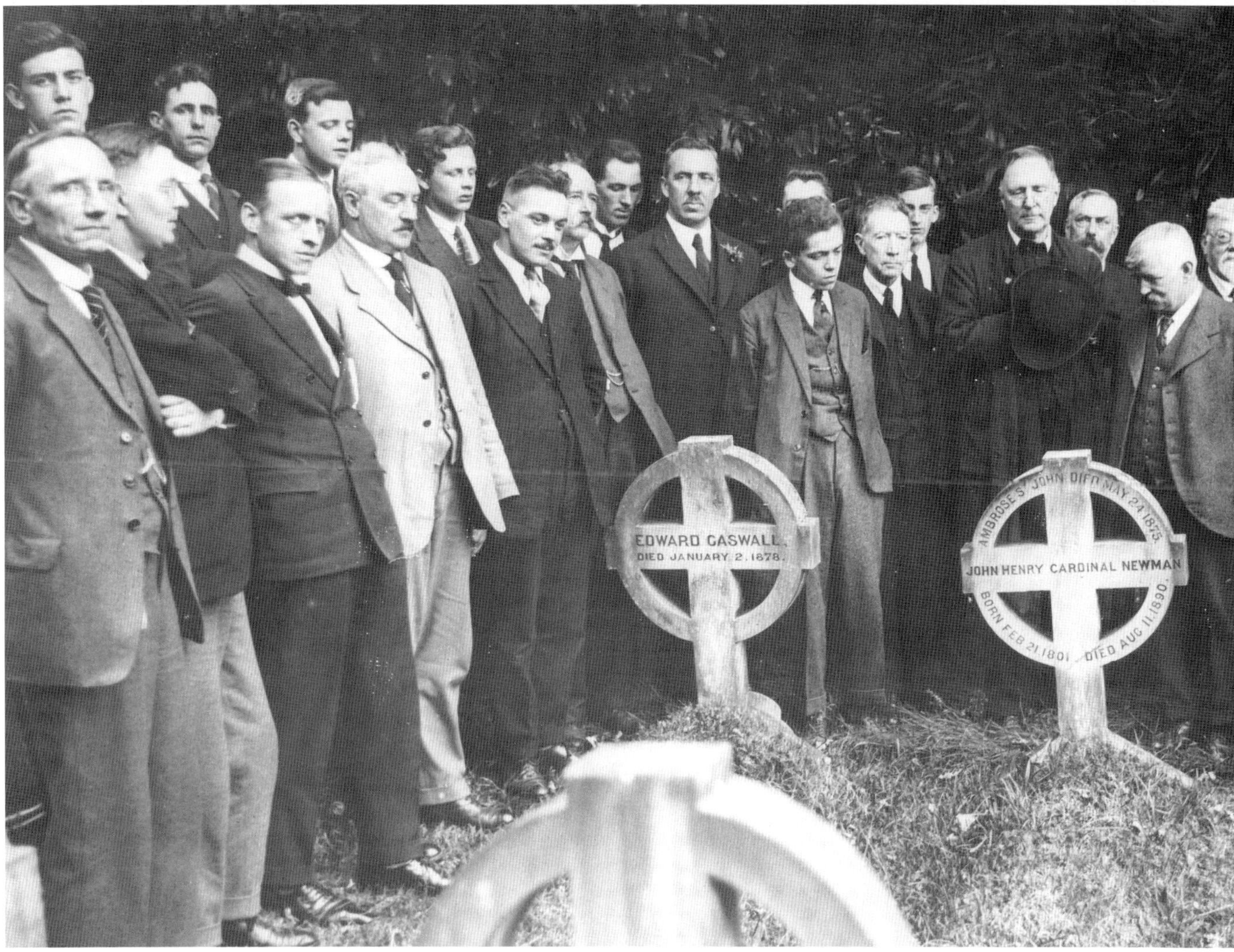

A solemn moment of reflection and prayer at the gravesides of Cardinal Newman and Ambrose St. John during an annual pilgrimage to the site at the cemetery at Rednal Hill near Birmingham in 1925. It was Newman's profound wish that he be buried with his lifelong friend Ambrose St. John, who converted to Catholicism at the same time as Newman. On the 22nd January 1991 Pope John Paul II confirmed the judgment of the Congregation for the Causes of Saints that John Henry Newman had practiced the theological and moral virtues "to a heroic degree", a pronouncement that opened the cause for his sainthood. A miracle attributed to Newman's intercession is currently under scrutiny by the Vatican.

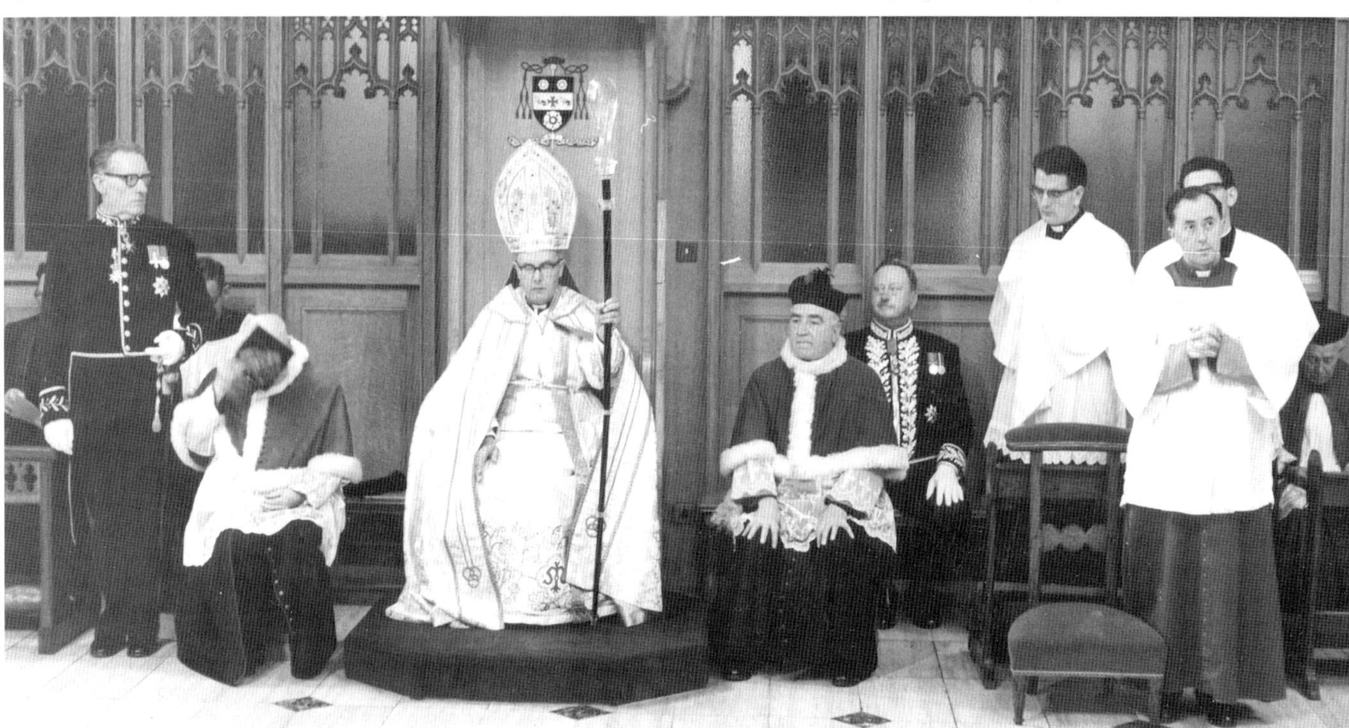

Bishop William Gordon Wheeler is enthroned at Leeds Cathedral on 27th June 1966.

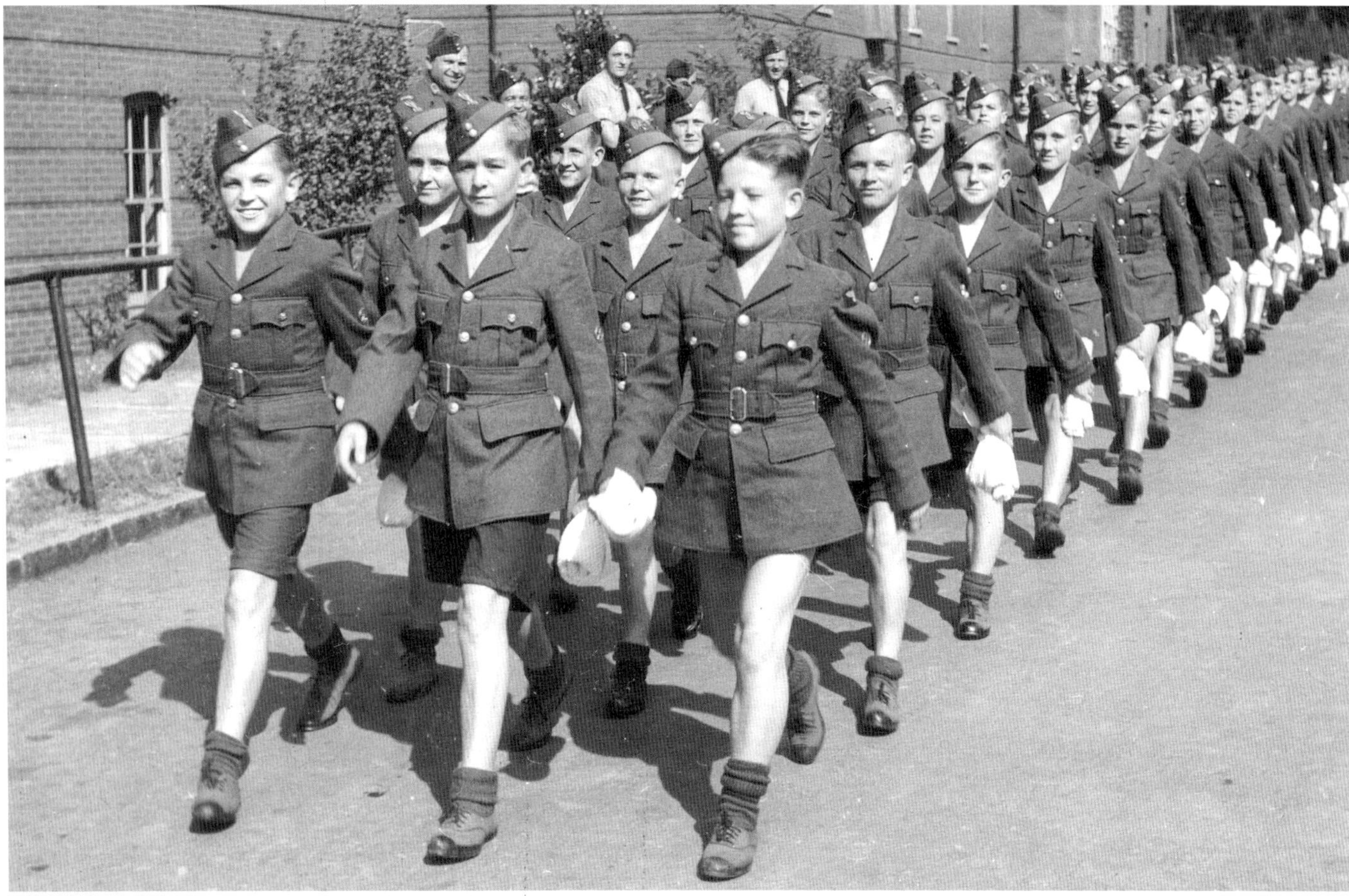

"Polish boys from Siberian ice-fields and Turkestan marshes – boys who before they had reached their teens were left alone in the world and saved their lives only by using their own wits in the midst of war-created chaos – are among this smart, happy-looking section of a junior apprentice wing of the RAF in Great Britain. They reached safety here, 204 of them, after travelling thousands of miles in the worst conditions in the wake of the Polish army. With home gone, parents dead and all traces of birth certificates vanished, many of them do not even know their own ages. In Britain they are learning to be good Poles, efficient airmen and mechanics and, with regular religious instructon, good Catholics." From *The Universe*, 22nd October 1943.

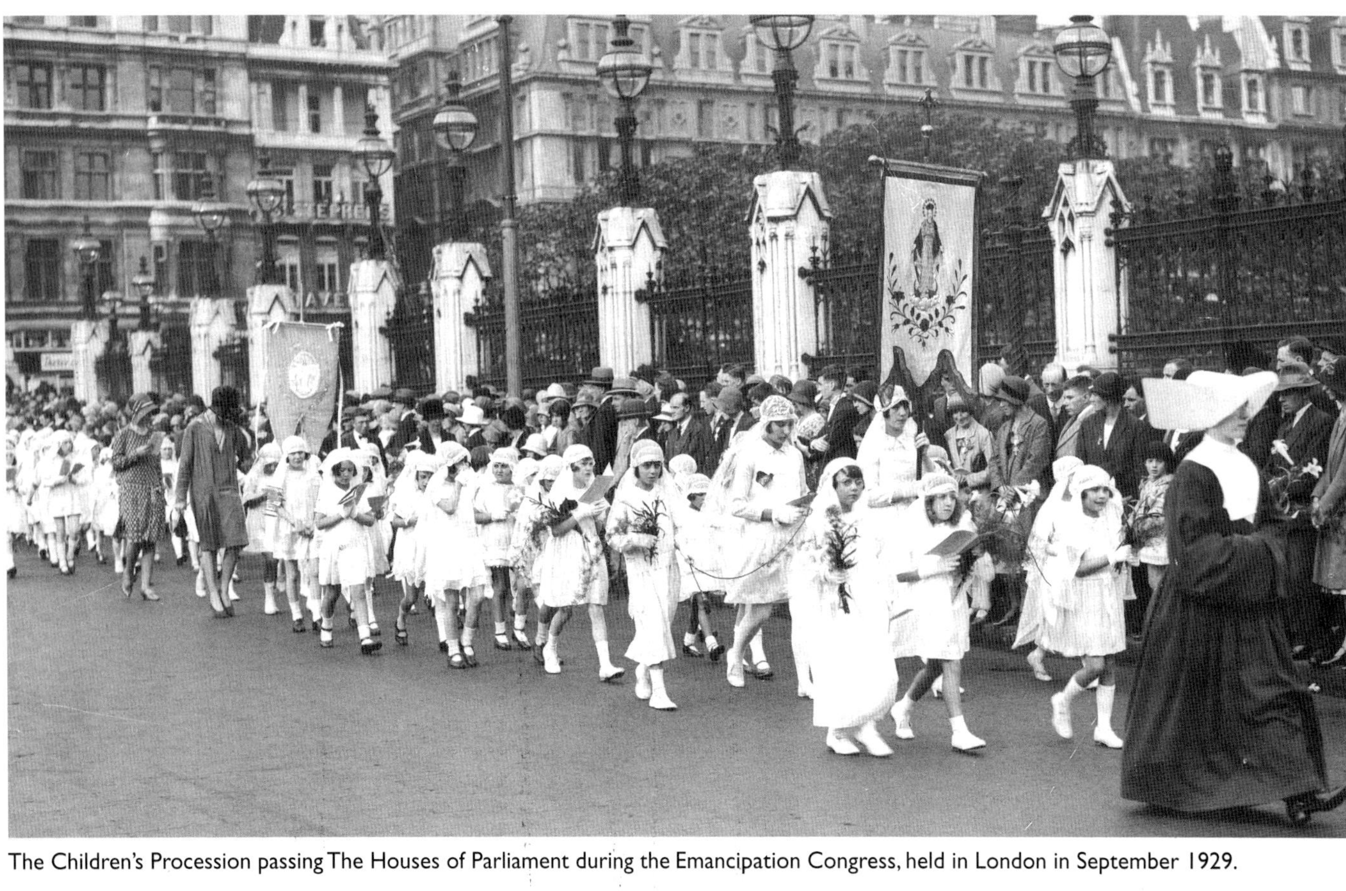

The Children's Procession passing The Houses of Parliament during the Emancipation Congress, held in London in September 1929.

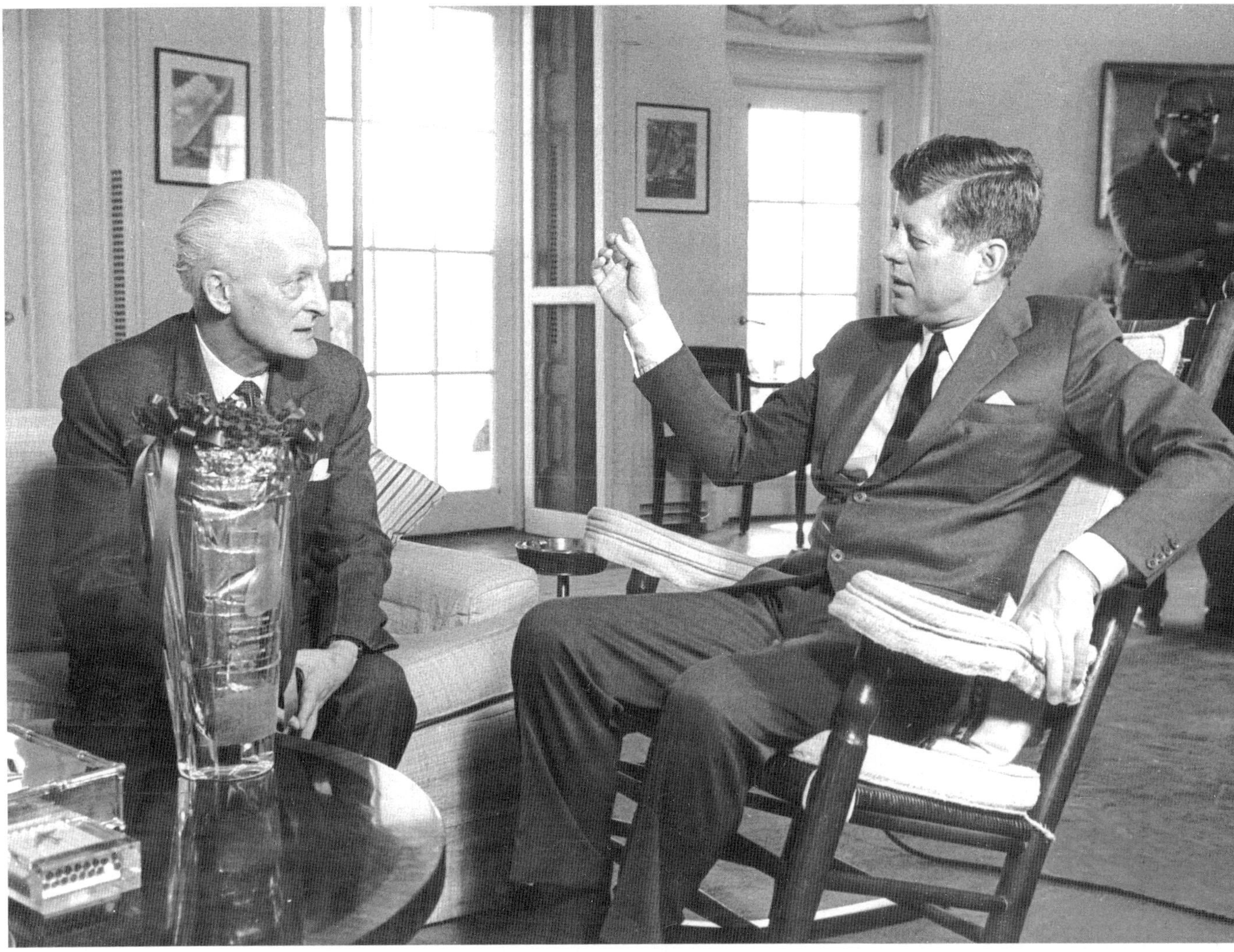

Washington DC. Irish Ambassador Thomas J. Kiernan calls at the White House on March 15 1963, for the envoy's annual St.Patrick's Day delivery of good wishes - and potted shamrocks. He called two days early because the president was leaving later that afternoon for Palm Beach, Florida.

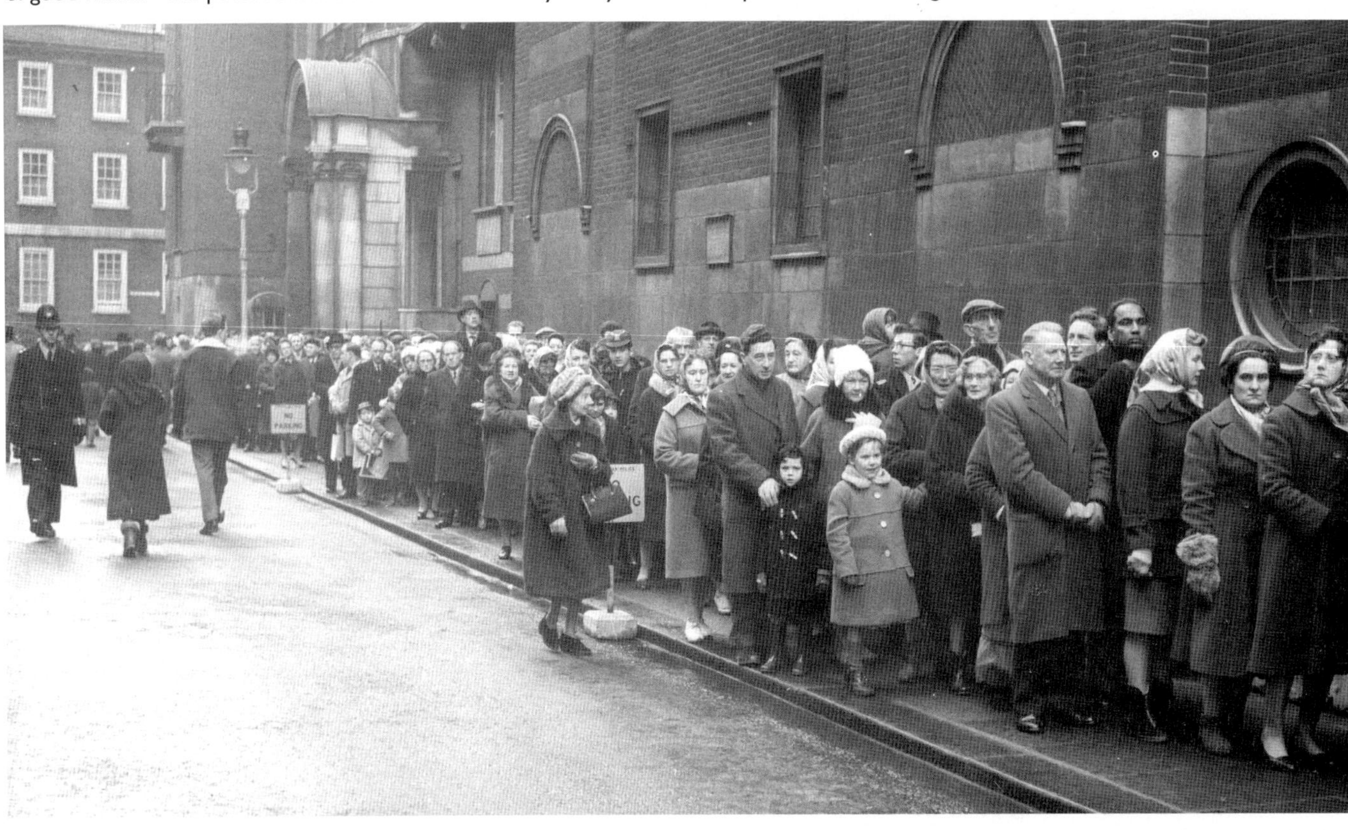

Some of the faithful are pictured outside London's Westminster Cathedral on 27th January 1963, where they were waiting to file past the body of William Cardinal Godfrey, Archbishop of Westminster, who had died the previous week.

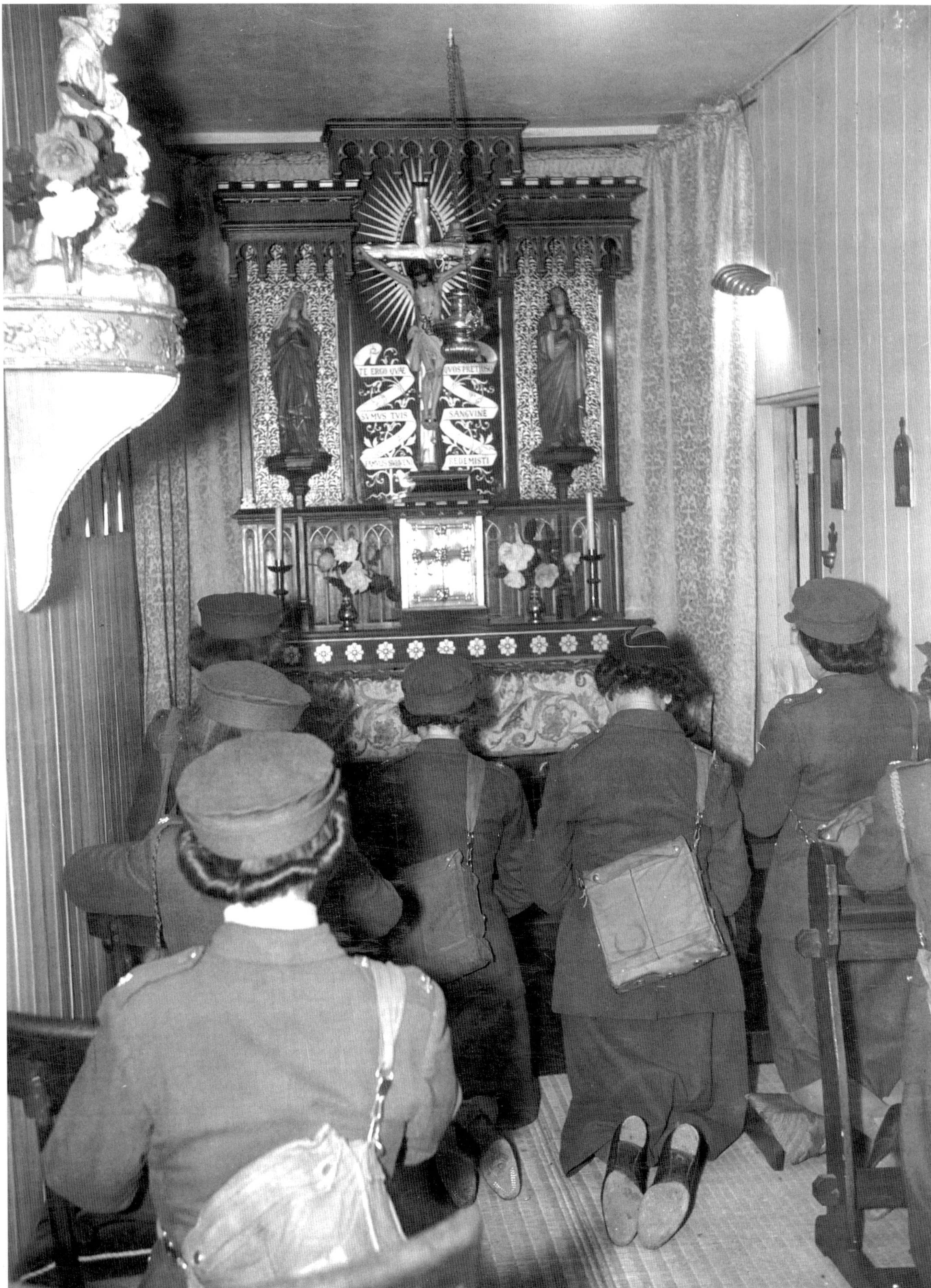

A quiet corner of the Catholic Women's League Belgrave Service Women's Club near London's Victoria station gives women at war an opportunity to pray for peace in July 1942. The club was opened by Cardinal Hinsley.

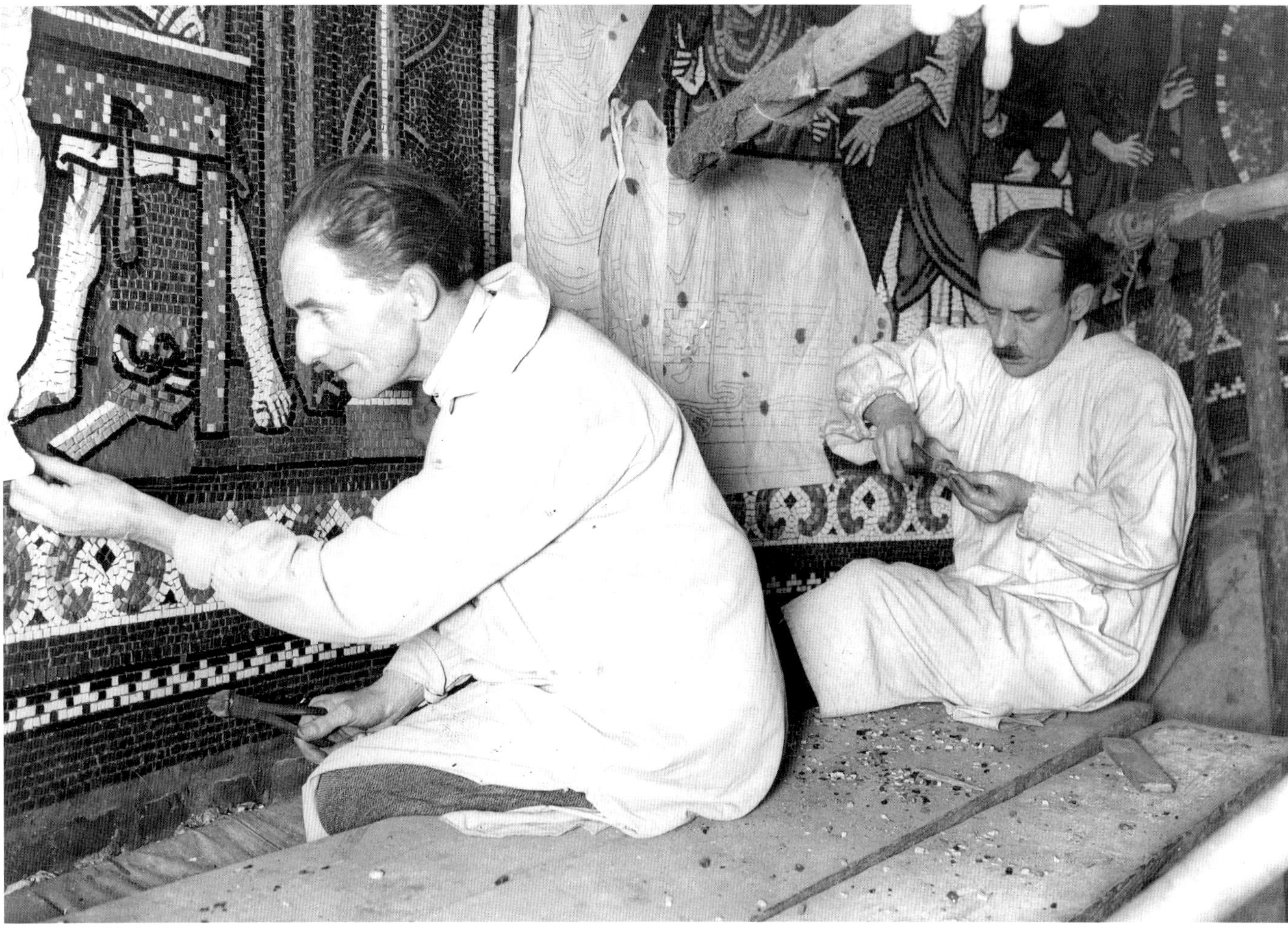

Artists at work covering with glass mosaic the dome of the apse in the Chapel of Our Lady at Westminster Cathedral in March 1931. The artist on the right is identified as Mr. Thomas Josey.

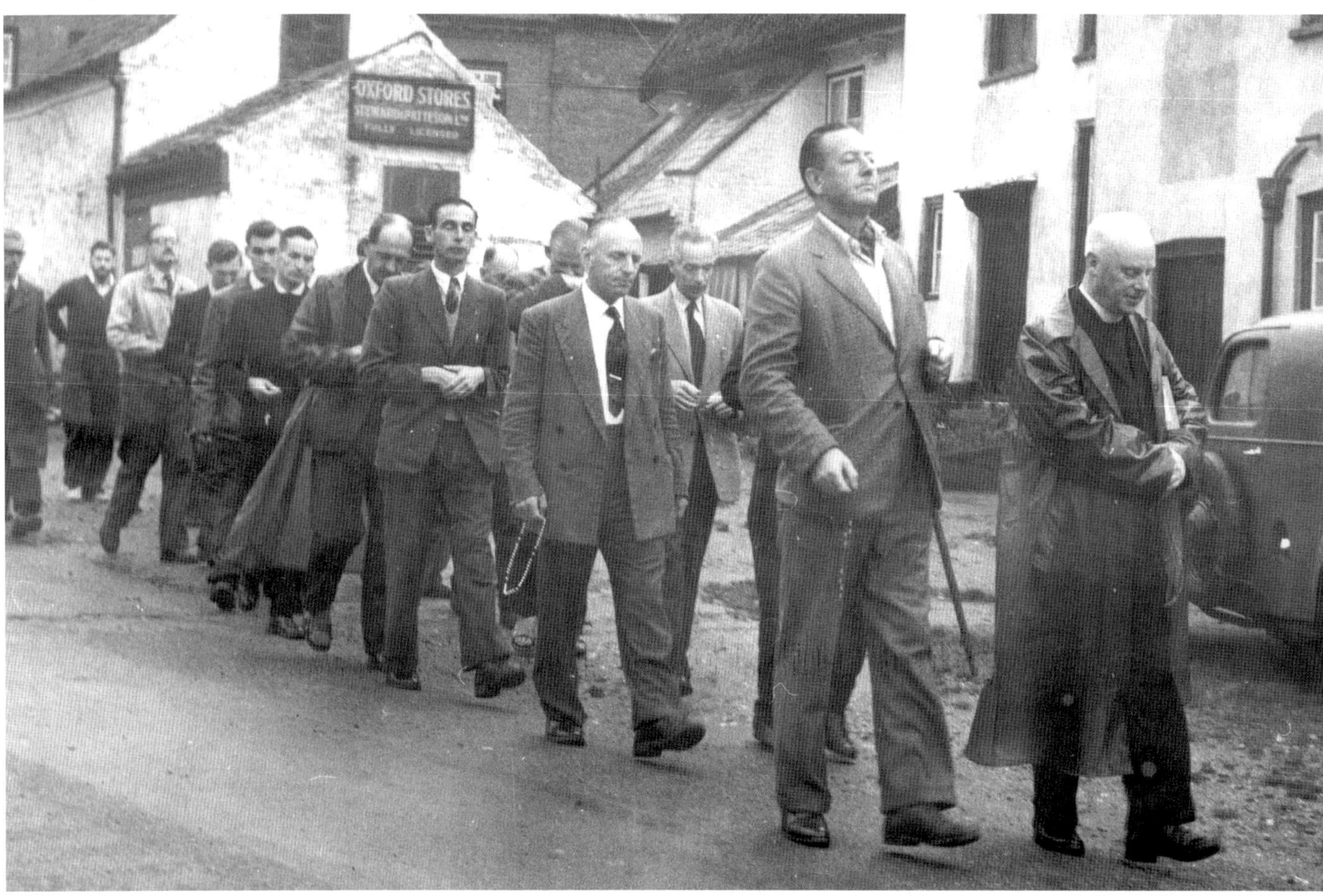

Catholic men leaving the Friday market, Walsingham, in procession during Walsingham Week in 1957.

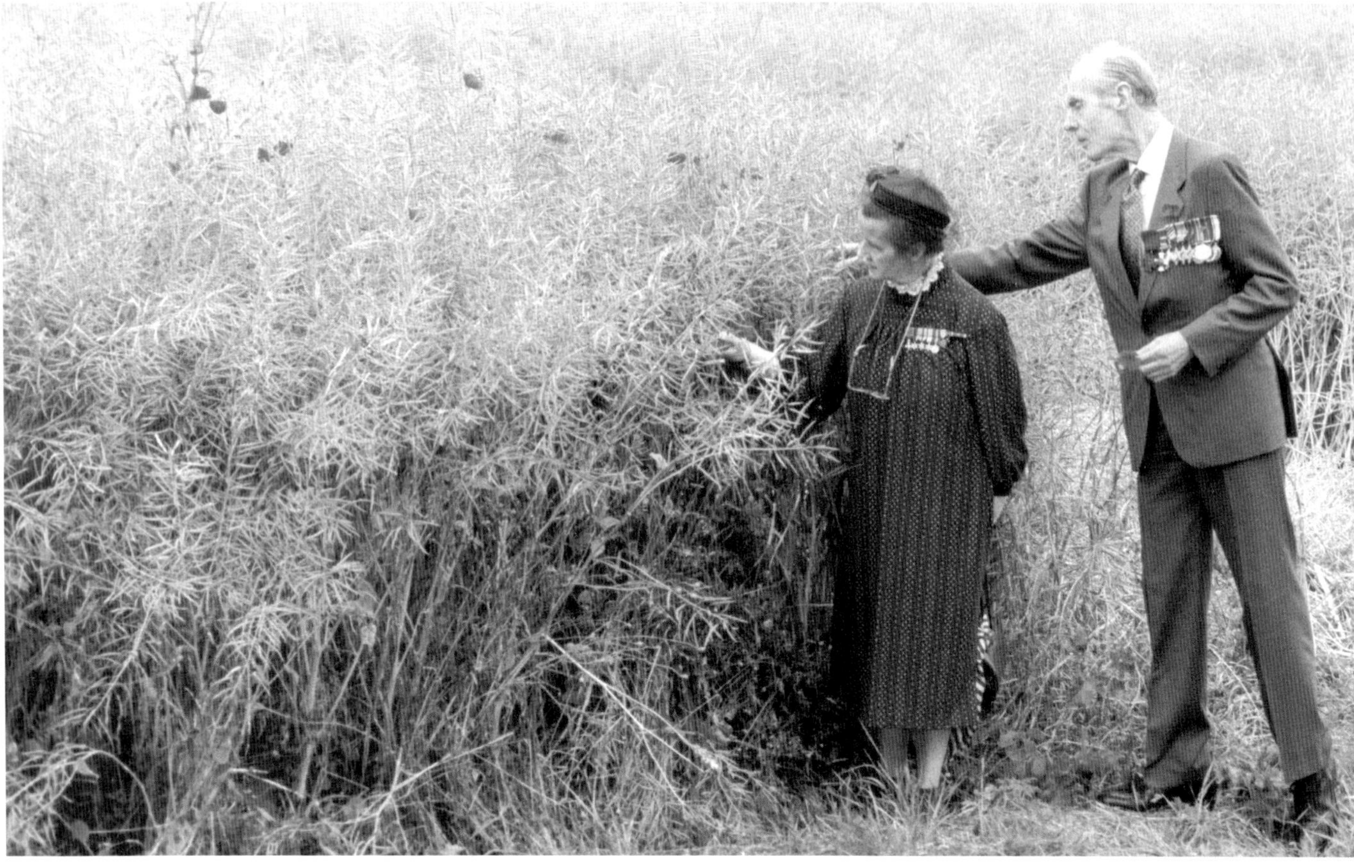

World War Two hero Group Captain Leonard Cheshire, later Lord Cheshire, with his wife Lady Ryder, walk among the poppies near the Lochnagar Crater on the Somme in July 1989.

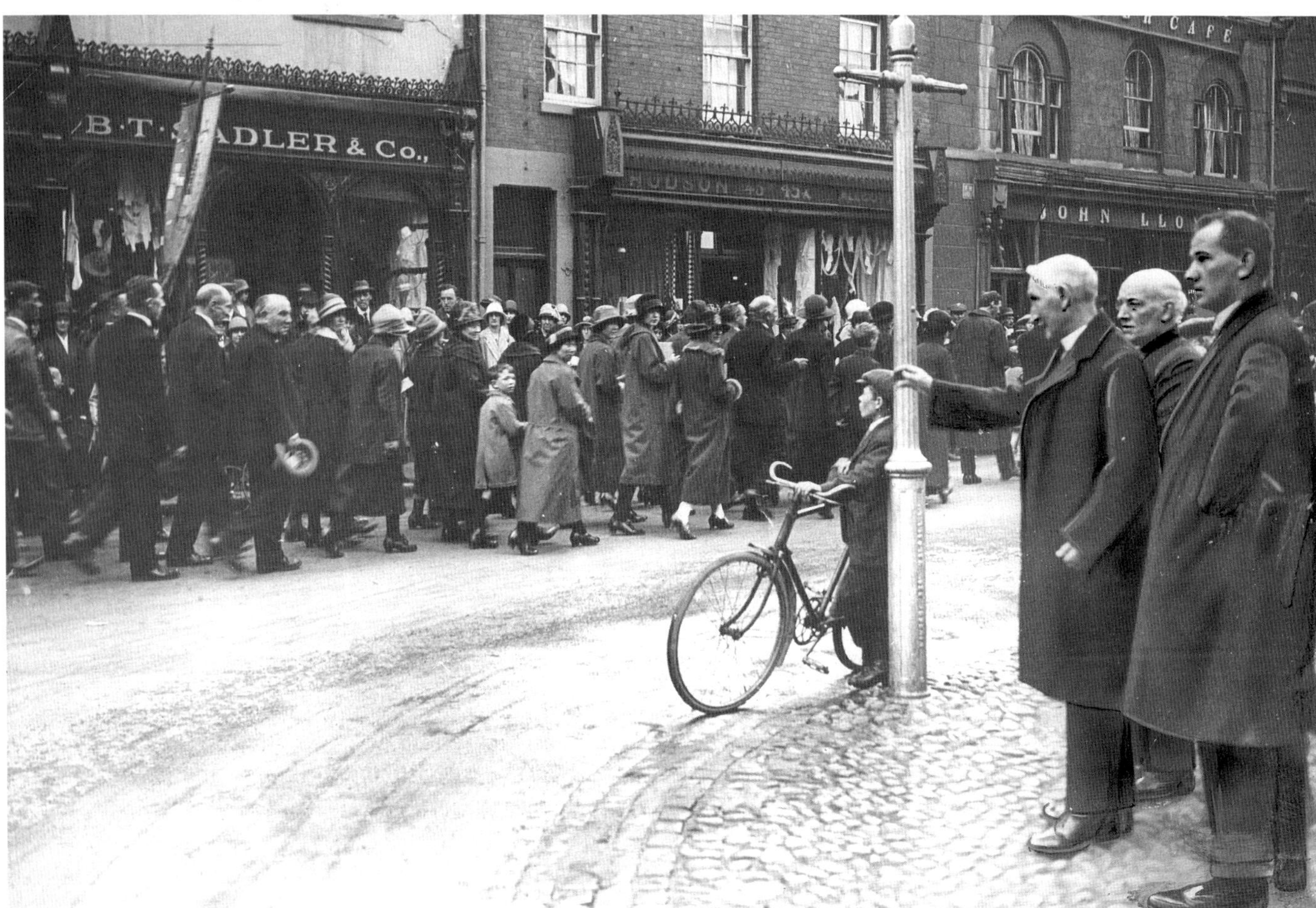

Sadly this picture is undated, but it shows Archbishop McIntyre of Birmingham blessing pilgrims as they passed through the market square, Lichfield, during the Midlands Catholic Pilgrimage to the town. John McIntyre was appointed Archbishop of Birmingham on 16th June 1921, and resigned on 17th November 1928, remaining Emeritus Archbishop until his death on 21st November 1935.

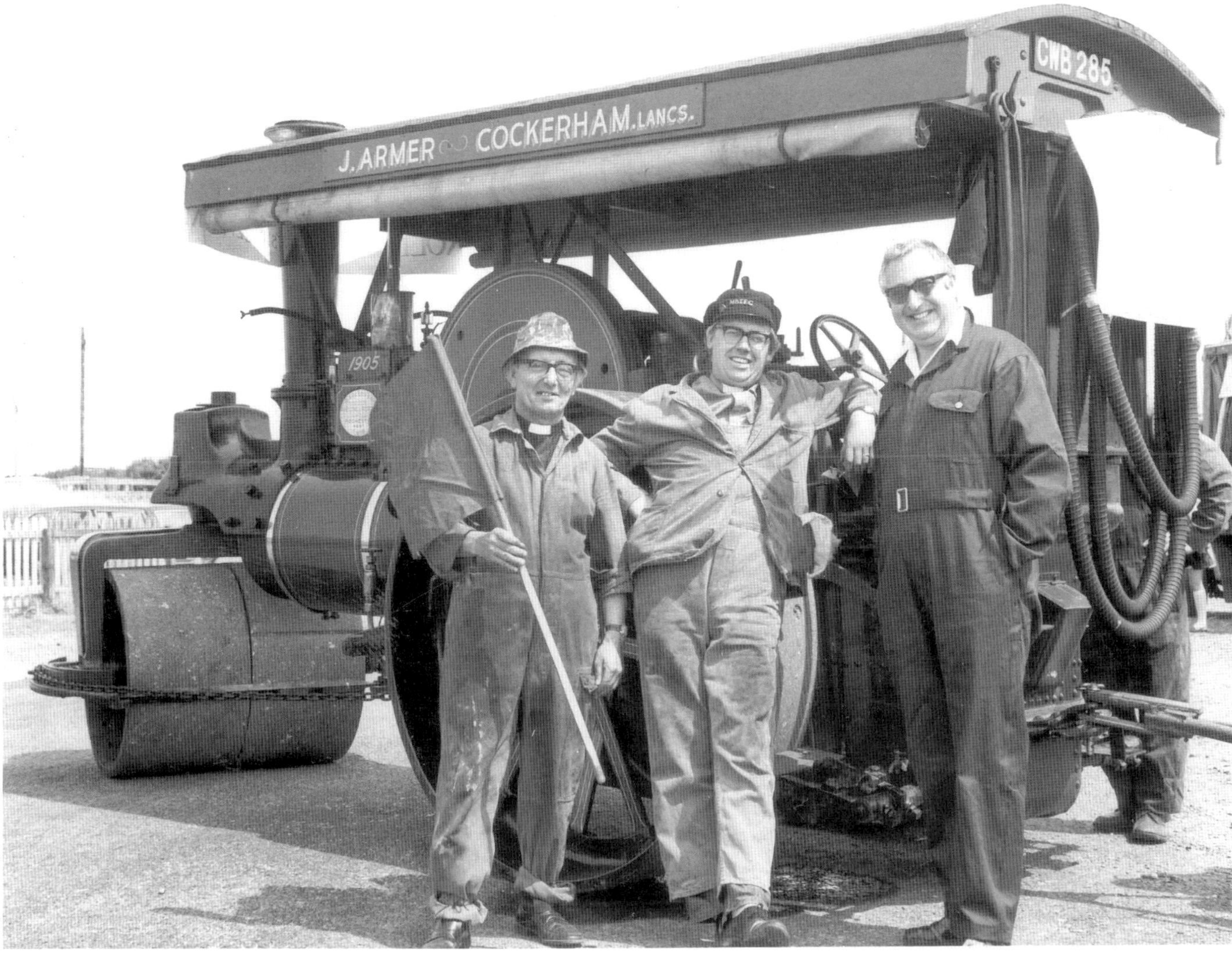

Clergy at Knott End, near Blackpool donned overalls and dressed as workmen during the Preesall Gala in August 1976. The Rev. R.F. Jackson, Vicar of Preesall (centre) drove a steam roller (borrowed from a friend), assisted by the Rev. H. C. Griffiths, United Reformed Church (left) and Fr. Bernard Cochrane, Catholic parish priest of St. Bernard's, Knott End. The venture was an extension of their normal monthly fraternal when they had an early service and breakfast together.

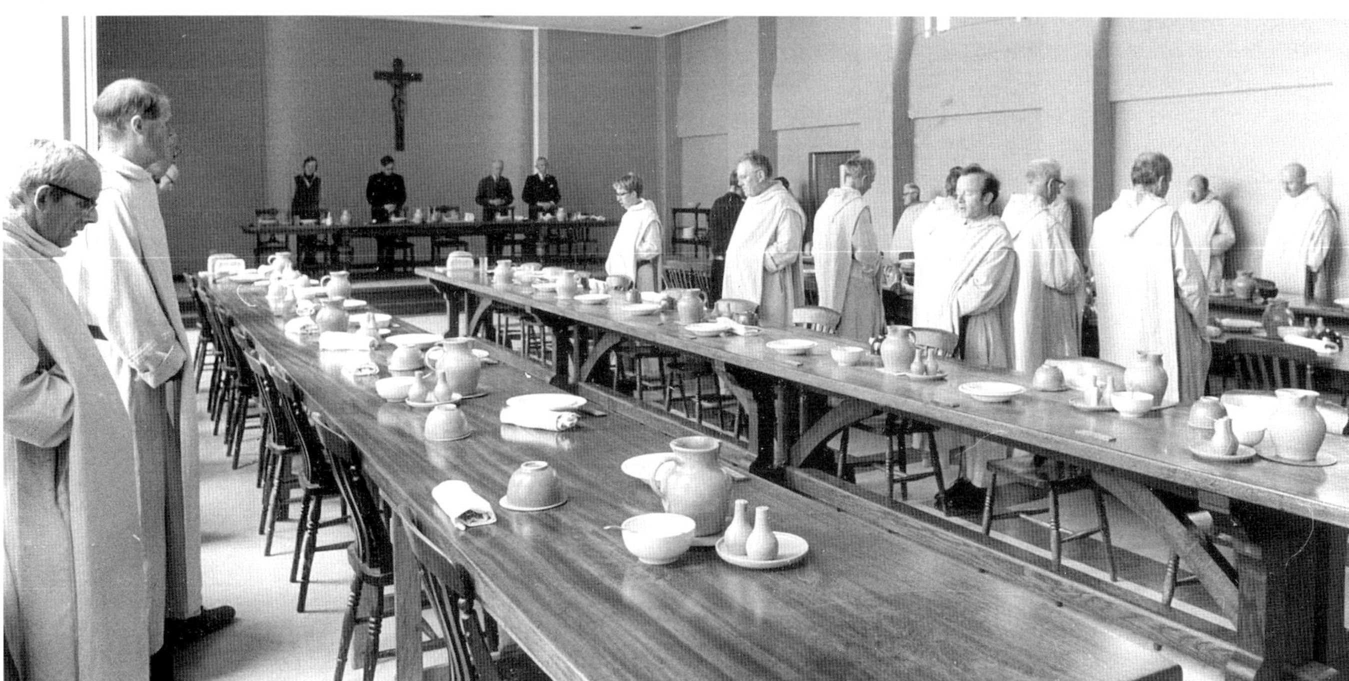

Lunchtime in the refectory of the newly completed £500,000 Prinknash Abbey, near Gloucester in April 1972. The new monastery, which became home to 37 Benedictine monks, replaced an old Tudor house, and boasted "central heating and shaver sockets in the cells" according to *The Universe*. The monastery was built by the monks themselves, with 2,500 tons of Cotswold stone.

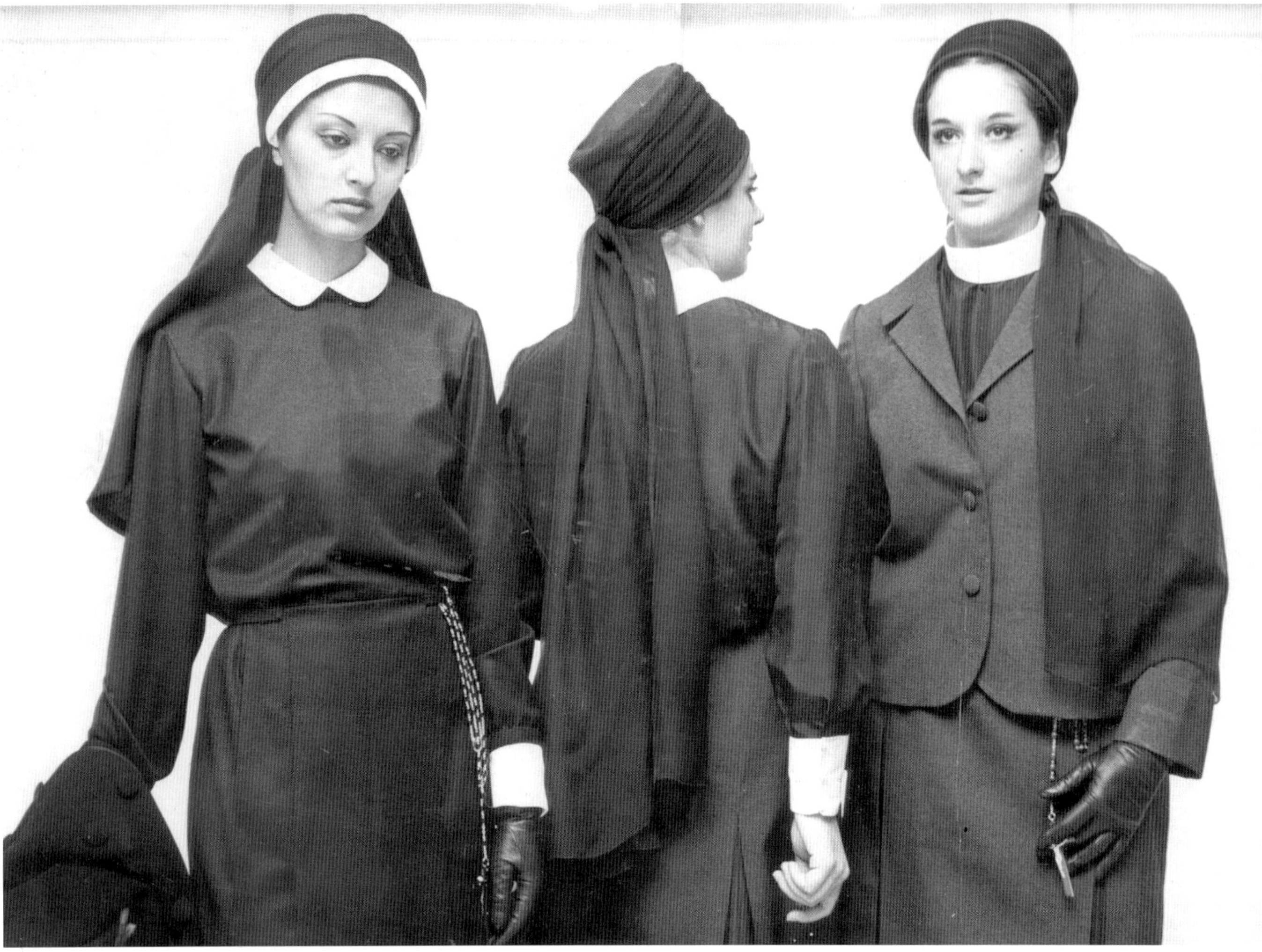

An unusual fashion show took place in August 1965 at the well known Rome fashion house of Fontana, just off the Piazza di Spagna. To quote the *Universe* article that appeared alongside this picture: "Nun's habits were presented, in view of the reforms being studied by the various orders. Thirty nuns from various congregations were present. The Fontana sisters themselves, one of whom had a daughter who recently became a nun, presented two models. A third was designed by a French fashion designer. The line of the habits is severe, but the designers demonstrated that severity and elegance can go together. The predominant colour was dark grey, with white trimmings. Strached veils have disappeared, and the skirt no longer touches the ground, but is designed so as to make it easy to drive a car. The nuns present suggested a few modifications, but on the whole they judged the models to be practical."

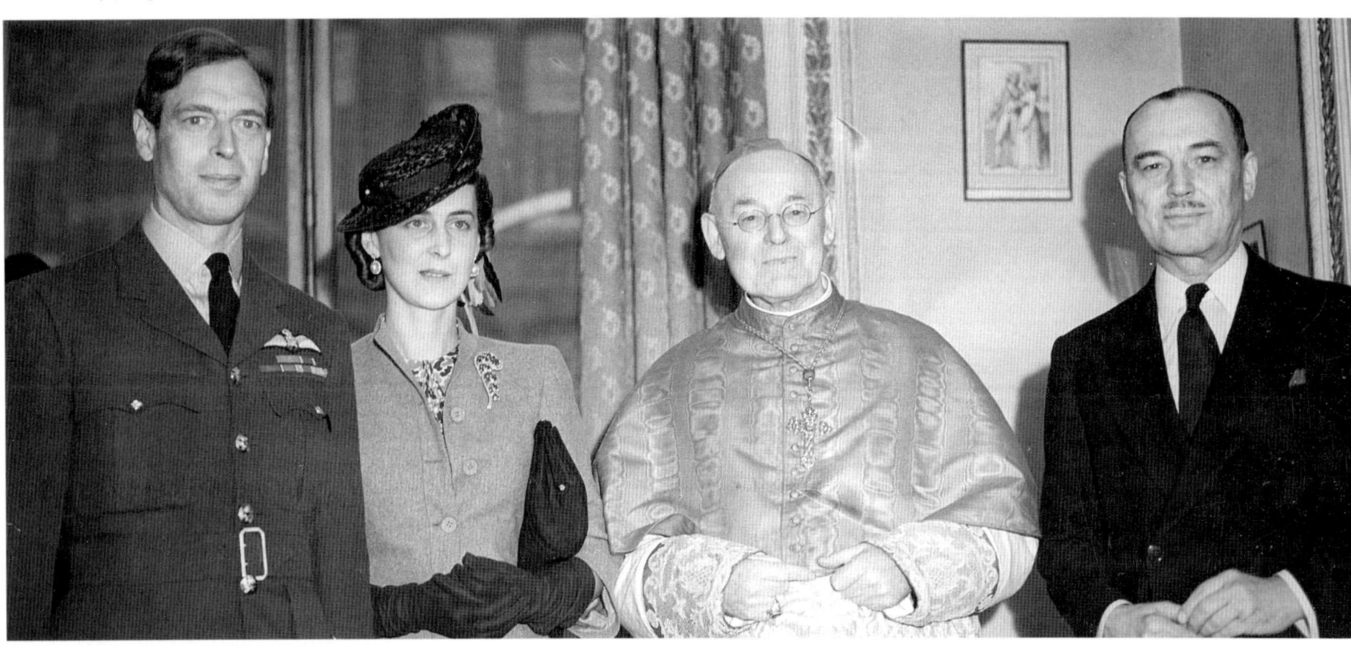

The Duke and Duchess of Kent pictured with Cardinal Hinsley and Lord Lloyd (Chairman of the British Council) at a reception after the opening of the Ognisko Polskie, the Polish House, in Prince's Gate, London in July 1940. The duke, who was younger brother to the king, was killed on 25th August 1942 while flying to Iceland on his duties as an Air Commodore of the Royal Air Force.

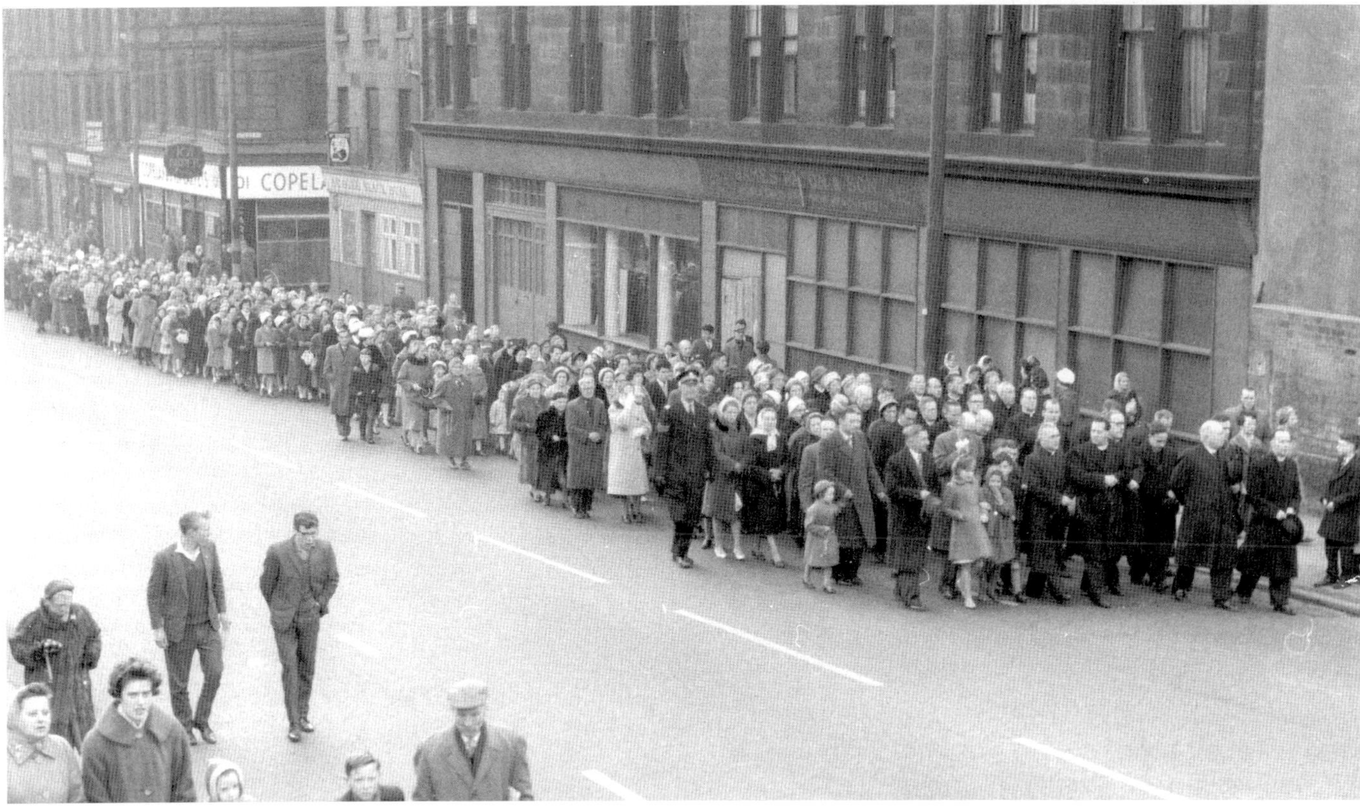

Glasgow crowds in procession up the city's High Street during the annual Blessed John Ogilvie procession in the mid 1960s.

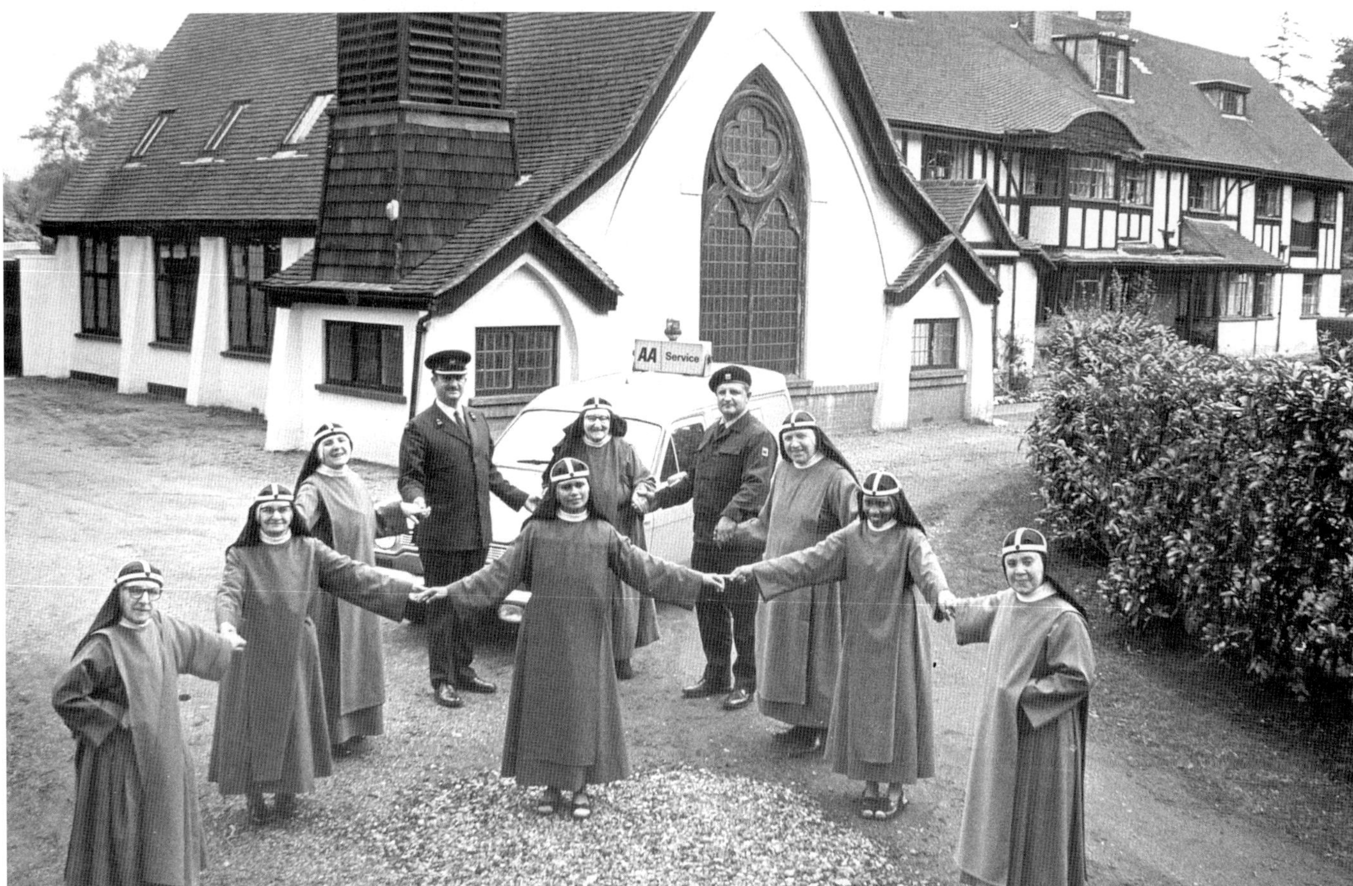

The Brigettine nuns at Iver Heath, Bucks, thought that their guest house was good enough to compete with the best and deserved to be more widely known. So, in May 1975, they wrote to the Automobile Association inviting them to come along and see for themselves. The AA sent along an inspector to investigate. He came back with a glowing report of what the nuns had to offer the weary traveller or people seeking a quiet holiday. No sparsely furnished cells, so beloved of romantic novelists. In this convent guest house, instead there are well furnished bedrooms with all mod cons, and meals of the highest standard. All this, plus extensive grounds, a fine library, colour television – and London just a half hour's drive away – for £2.75 a day for full board. And so this heavenly little spot is being recommended by the AA in its new Budget Guide to holiday accommodation. The community of eight, headed by Mother Seraphime, were very pleased to have qualified for ther AA accolade and were delighted to pose outside their guest house.

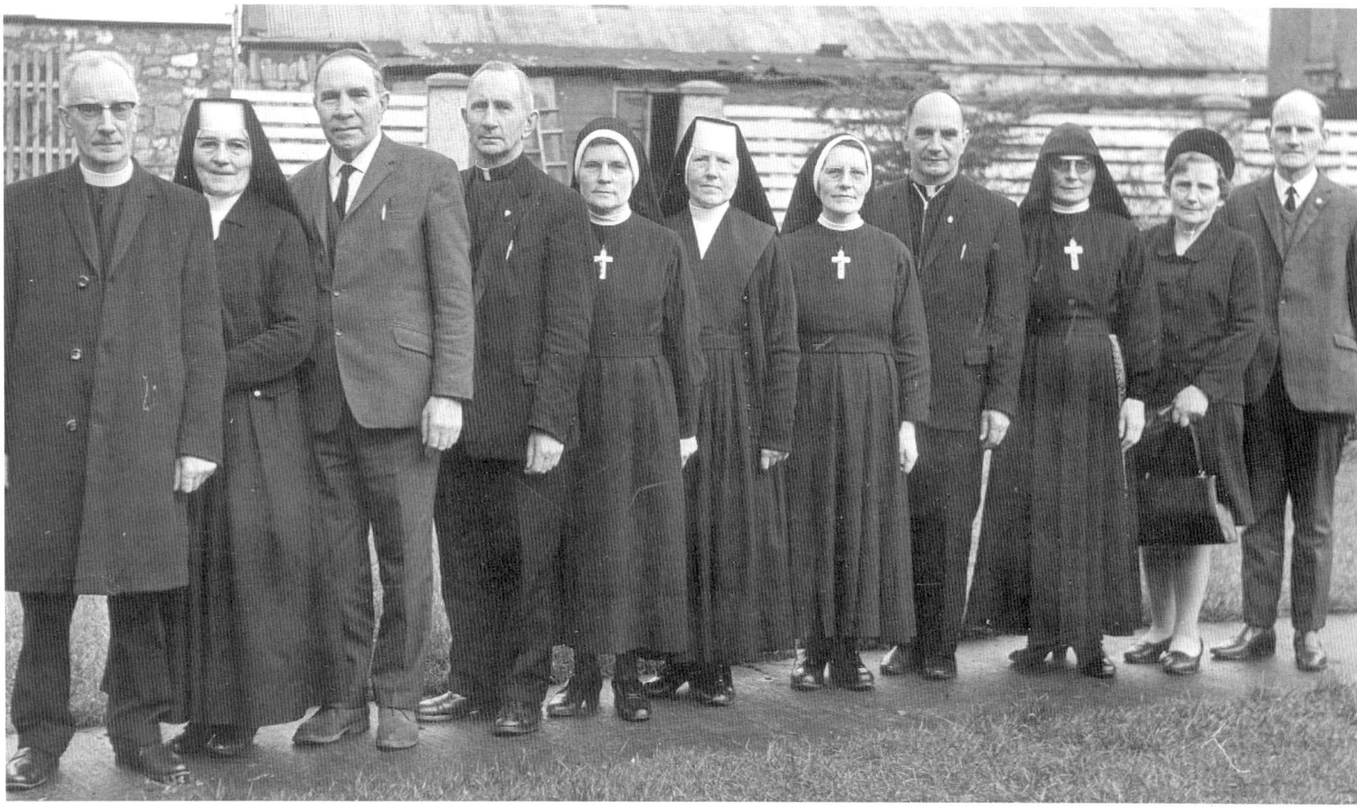

Eleven brothers and sisters – including three priests and five nuns – met for the first time in many years for the funeral of their mother, Mrs. Helena Bluett, of Kilmallock, Co. Limerick, in January 1970. Pictured from left: Fr. James Bluett, parish priest of Kilmeedy, Co. Limerick; Sr. Mary Clare, Sisters of Charity, Charleville, Co. Cork; Mr. Thomas Bluett, retired farmer, Kilmallock; Canon Patrick Bluett, parish priest of St. Mary's, Market Weighton, Yorks; Sr. Hilda, Irish Sisters of Charity, Dublin; Sr. Francis Therese, Buttevant, Co. Cork, Sr. Frances Bernadette, Chester; Fr. John Bluett, parish priest Good Shepherd, Downham, Kent; Sr. Magdalen Regis, St. Vincent's, Cork; Miss Joan Bluett, assistant matron, Barrington's Hospital, Limerick, and Mr. William Bluett, businessman, of Charville, Co. Cork.

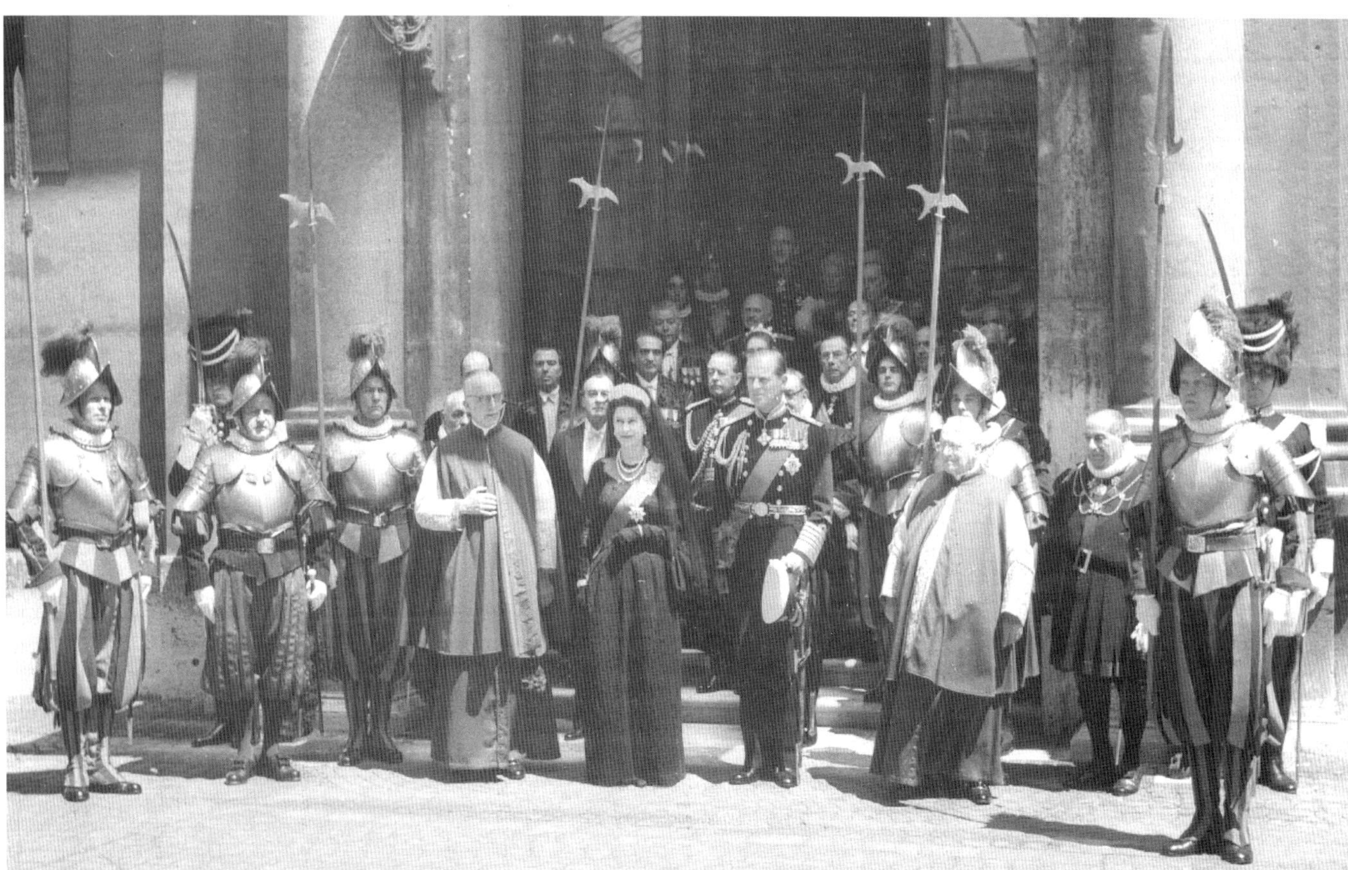

The Queen and the Duke of Edinburgh, followed by their entourage, leave St. Peter's Basilica, escorted by Swiss Guards, after their first visit to Pope John XXIII. The Queen wore a black lace gown and veil topped by a diamond tiara for her 20 minute historic meeting with the pontiff. The British royal couple were on a state visit to Italy.

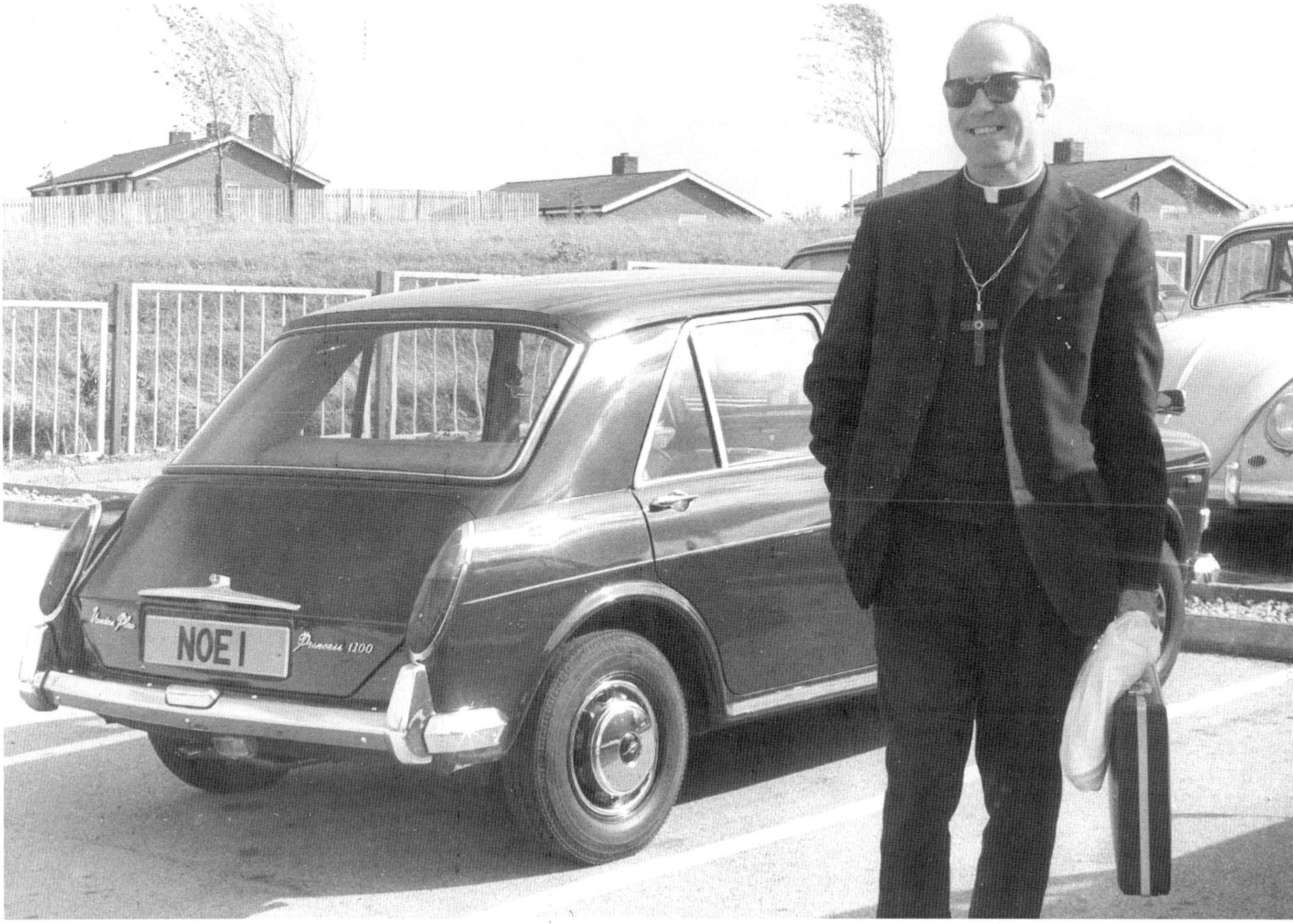

Sadly this photograph is undated, but it shows Bishop Derek Worlock arriving at Newman College, Birmingham. Note the very appropriate car registration number: NOE I. Derek Worlock was ordained to the priesthood in 1944 in Westminster Cathedral, and not long afterwards was appointed private secretary to Cardinal Griffin. He assisted successive cardinals for some 19 years. He attended every session of the Second Vatican Council between 1962 and 1965, the year in which he was appointed Bishop of Portsmouth. In 1976 he was appointed Archbishop of Liverpool. In January 1994 he was awarded the Freedom of the City of Liverpool. He was made Companion of Honour in the 1996 New Year's Honours List, but died of lung cancer four days after his 76th birthday, just a week before he was due to receive the honour.

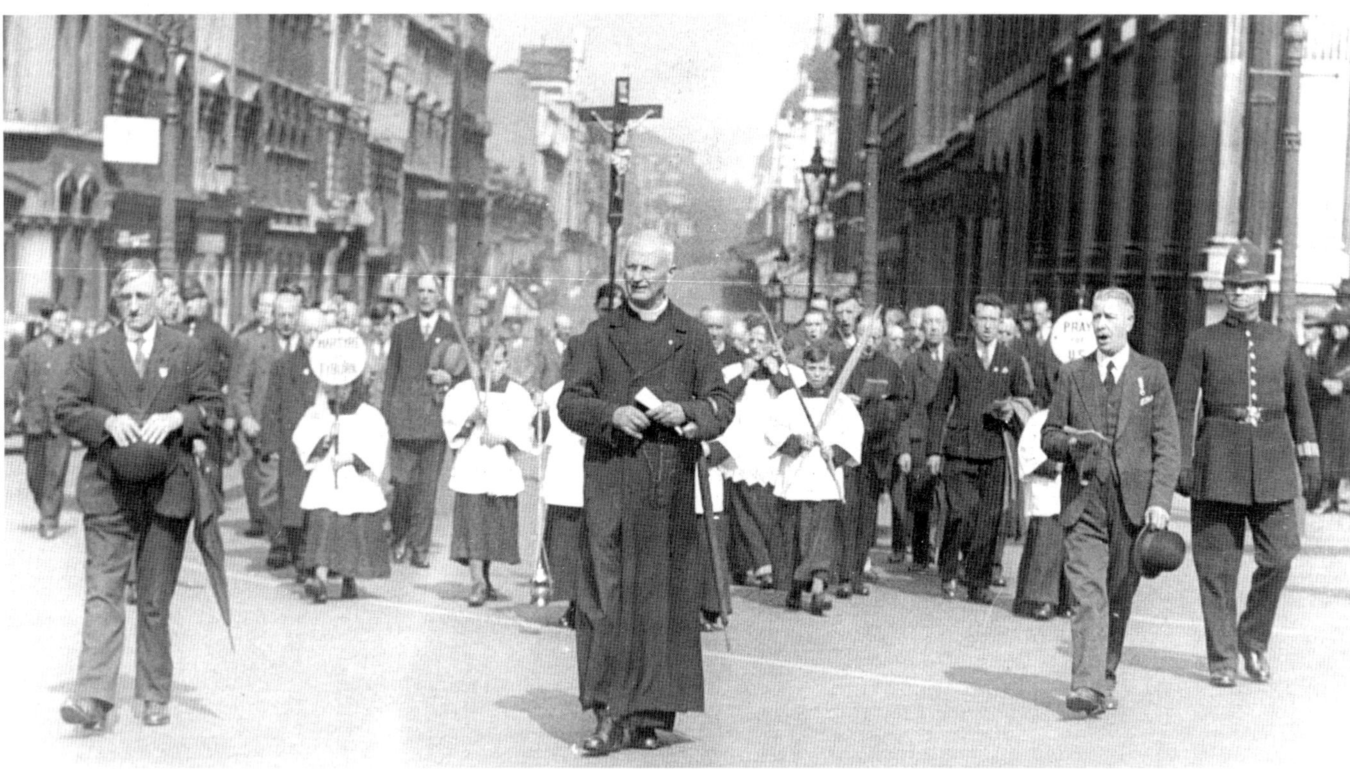

Father Filmer, Master of the Guild of our Lady of Ransom, with altar servers bearing the martyr's palms, leading the Tyburn Walk in May 1933.

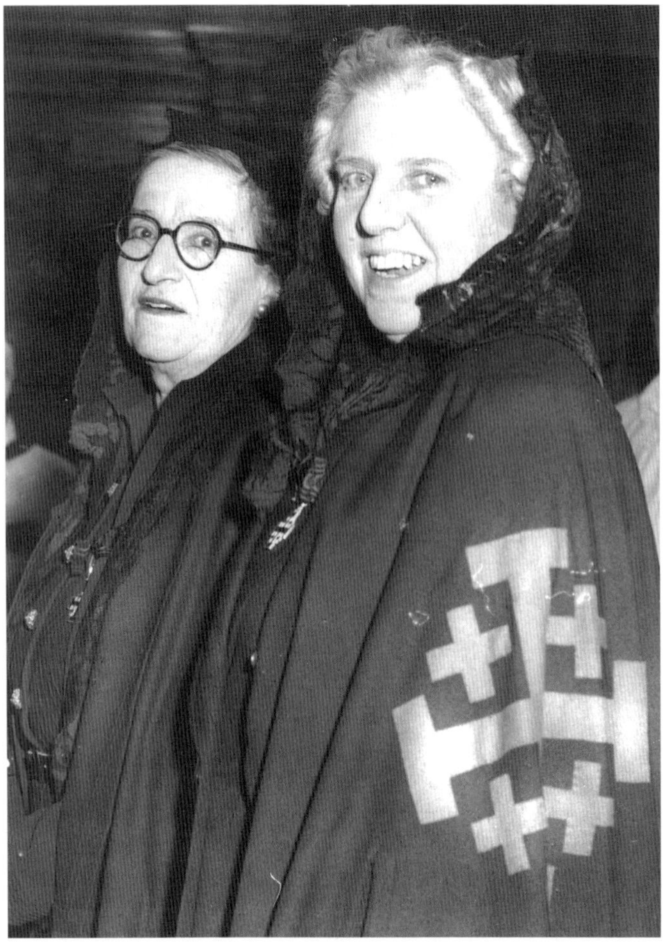

Two women received the title of Lady of the Holy Sepulchre of Jerusalem in Westminster Cathedral on 4th November 1955. Miss Holland was well known for her work with Lourdes pilgrimages, and Dr. Dorothy Makepeace was Senior Inspector at the Children's Department of the Home office.

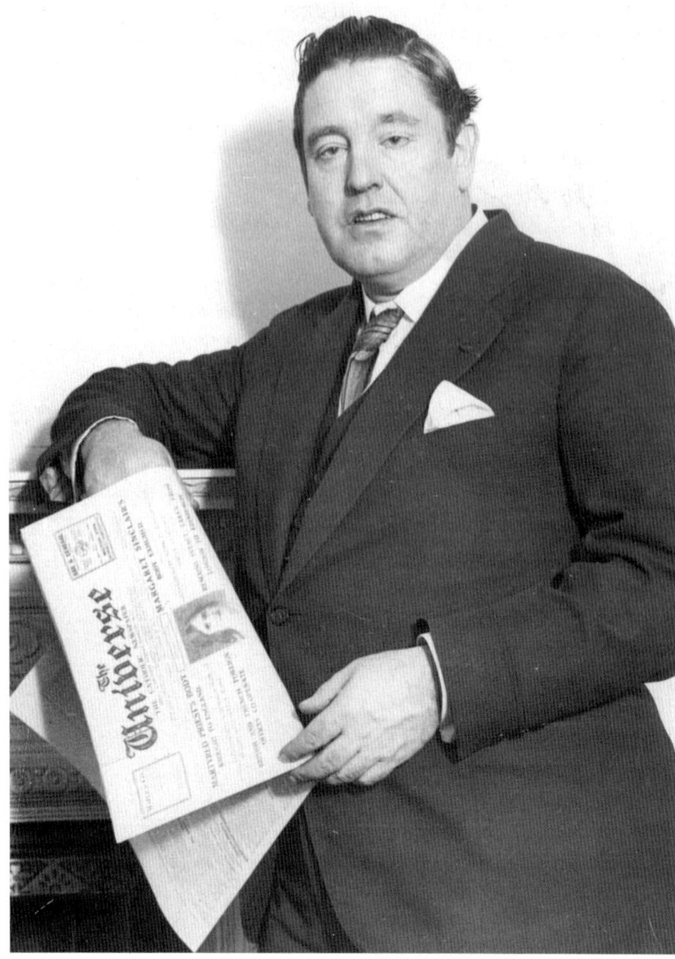

The great Irish tenor, Count John McCormack, reading his *Universe* before a concert performance in London in January 1928. The singer was a regular reader, and in December 1930 broke off from a world tour to sing for the staff of the newspaper at their 70 year celebratory dinner.

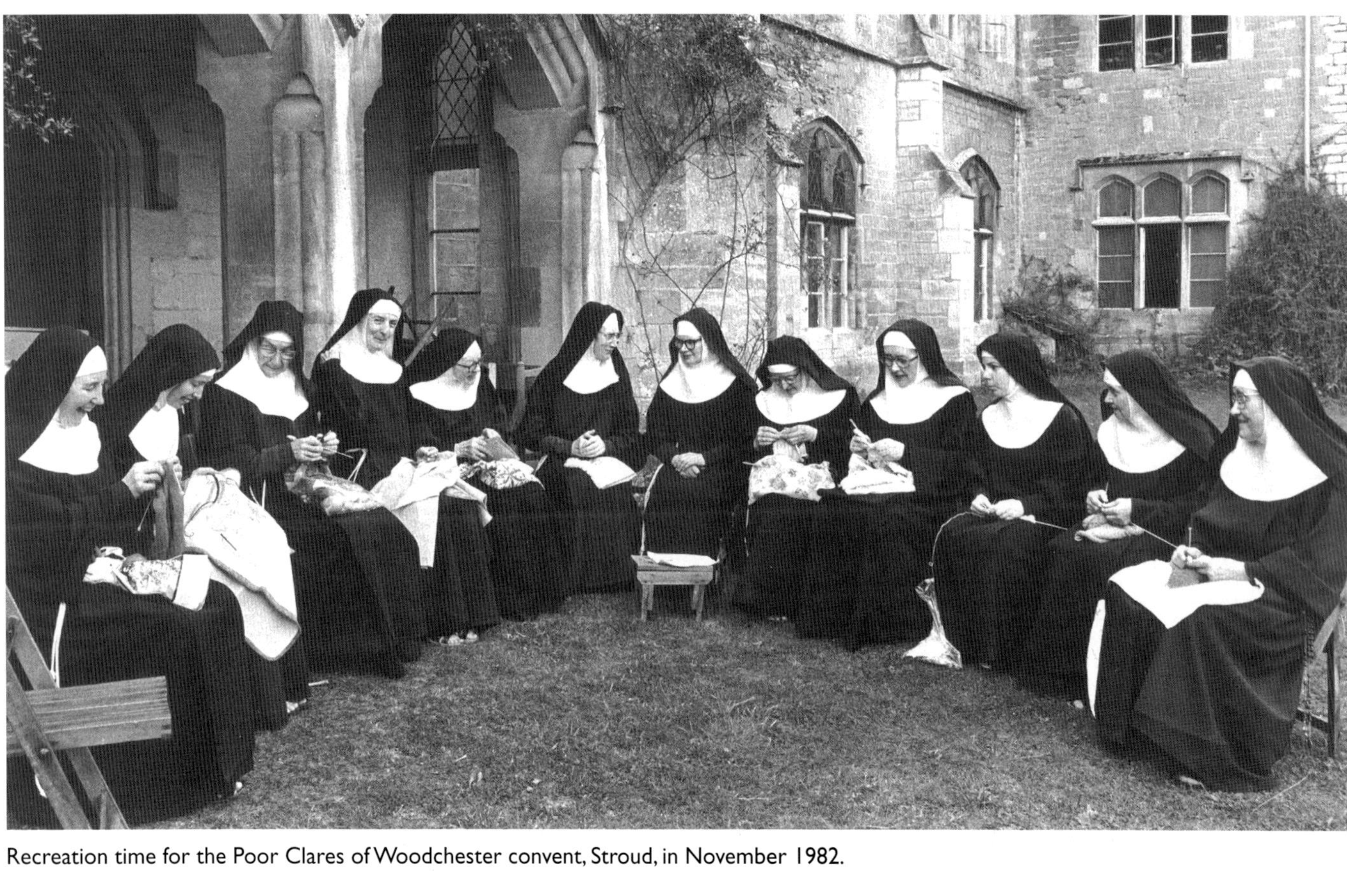

Recreation time for the Poor Clares of Woodchester convent, Stroud, in November 1982.

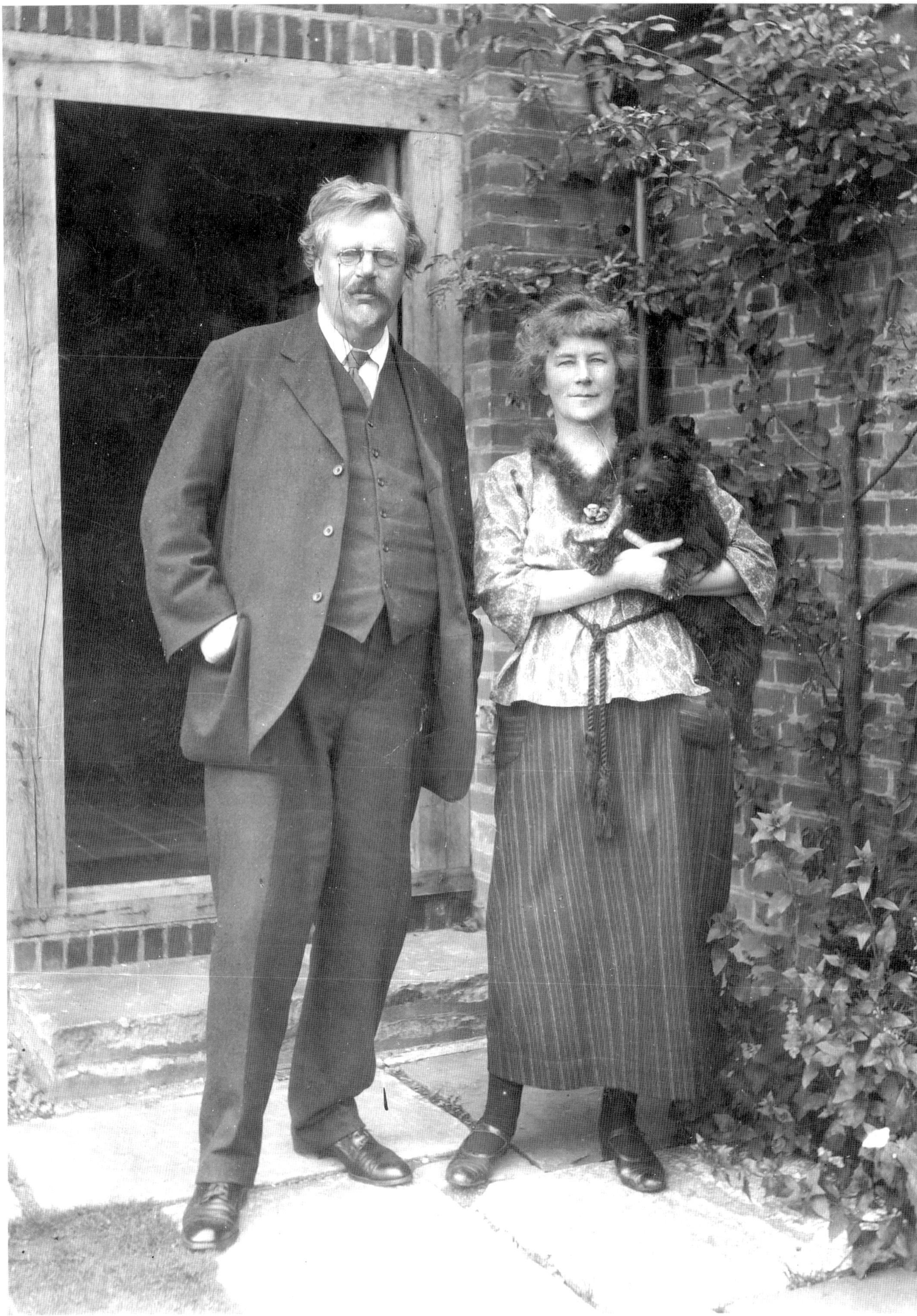

Mr. and Mrs. G.K. Chesterton pictured relaxing at home in December 1938.

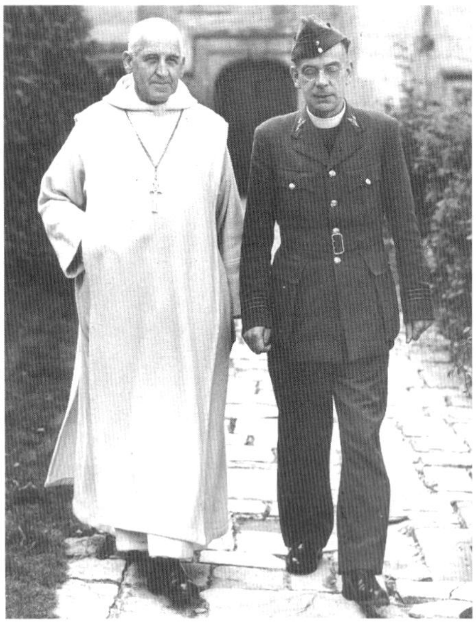

The Abbot of Prinknash, the Rt. Rev. Dom Wilfred Upson OSB, walks through the abbey gardens in May 1942 with Squadron Leader J. B. McHugh, otherwise Dom Brendan McHugh OSB, a member of the community who was serving as an RAF chaplain during the war.

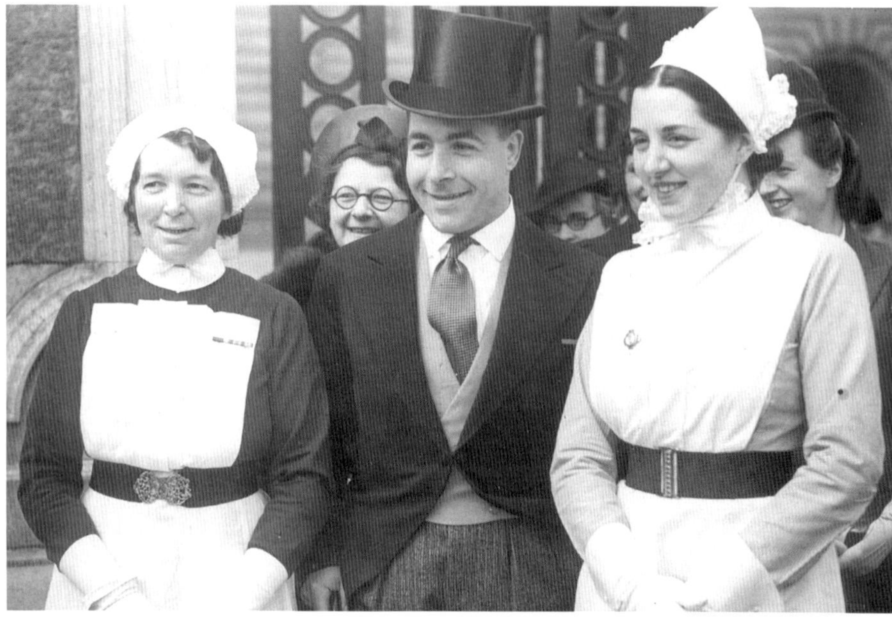

Three Catholic members of staff of the Royal London Chest hospital were decorated with the George Medal in May 1941 for bravery during an air raid. (From left) Miss Catherine McGovern, assistant matron, Dr. Andre Bathfield and Miss Patricia Marmion, staff nurse. Despite being wounded after a bomb demolished the in-patients' block they continued to treat and rescue staff hurt in the blast, and stayed to search the ruins for survivors.

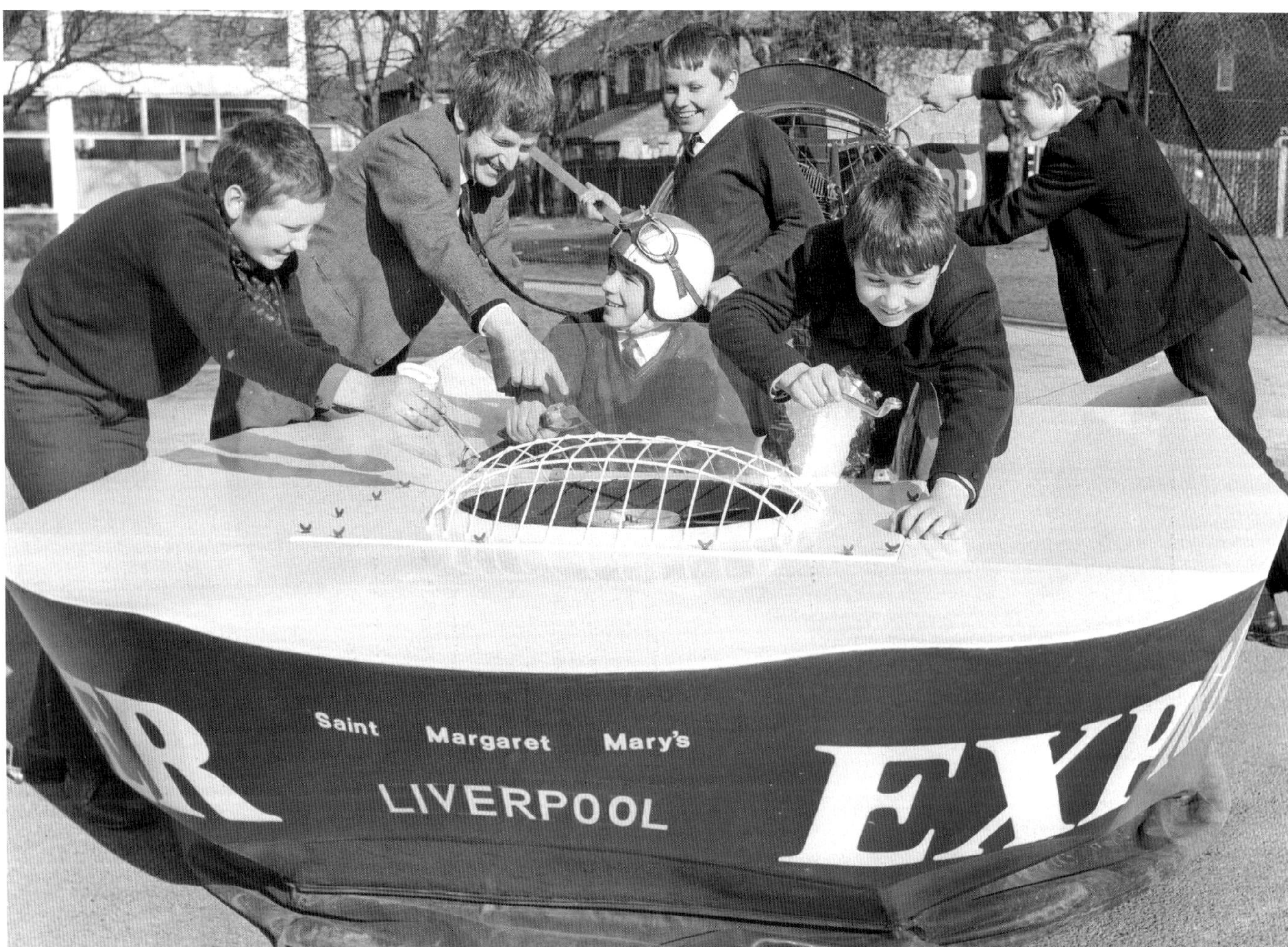

Two second-hand motor cycle engines powered this two seater hovercraft with a speed of 40 knots, built by boys at St. Margaret Mary's secondary school, Liverpool in March 1970. Built under the guidance of Mr. David Williams head of the school's technical department, it cost £100 and took 6,000 hours to build. Liverpool authority gave £75 towards materials and the school raised the rest. Built of marine plywood, the craft was 14ft long and 7ft wide and weighed 476lbs. The boys spent holidays, Saturdays and three to four nights a week working on it. Pictured putting the finishing touches to the craft are (left to right) Stephen Thomas, Mr. Williams, Anthony O'Toole, Bernard Gallagher, Geoff Dunne and Michael Williams.

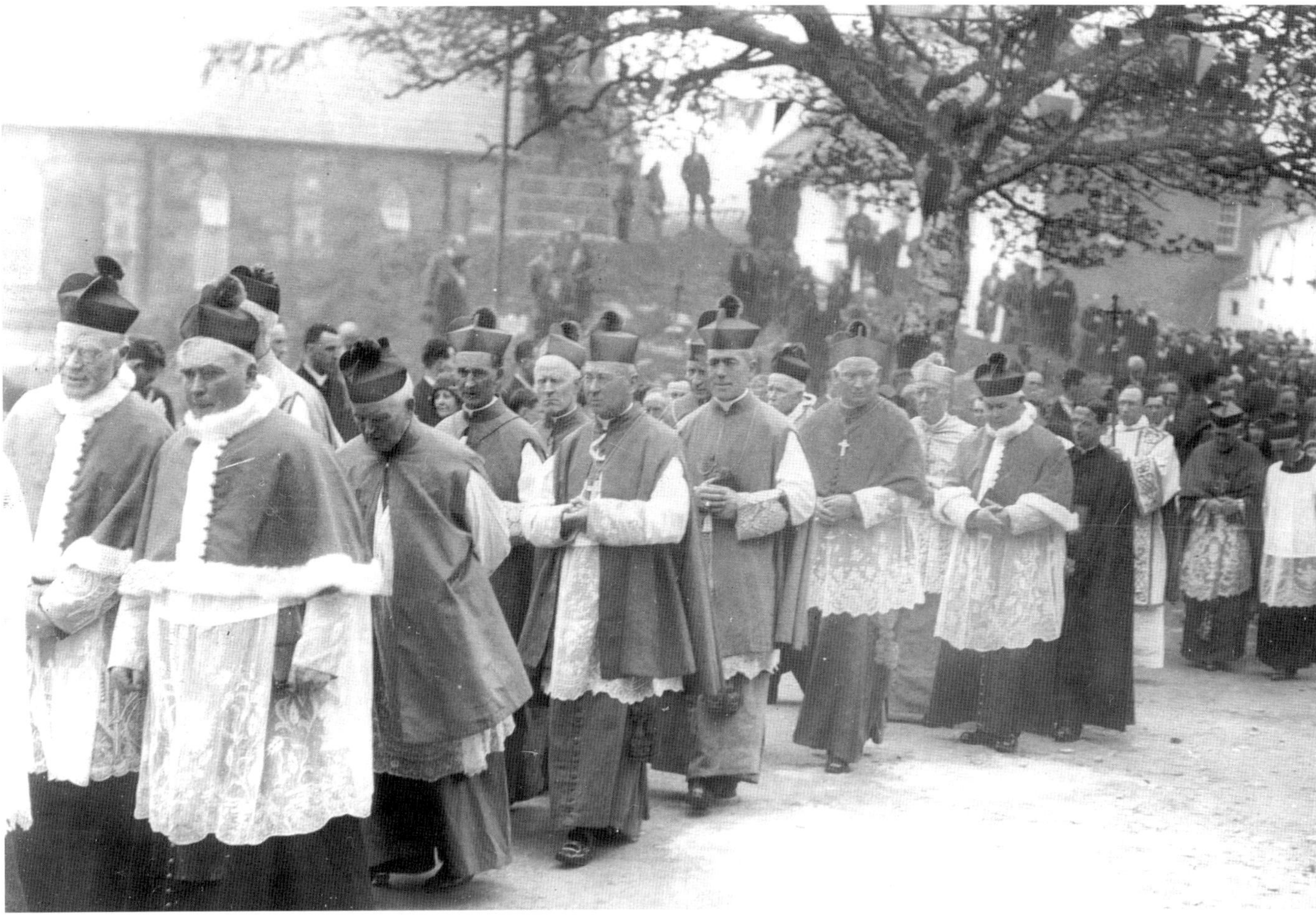

The bishops of Ireland seen walking in procession to a service to mark the consecration of a new church at Lough Derg in May 1931.

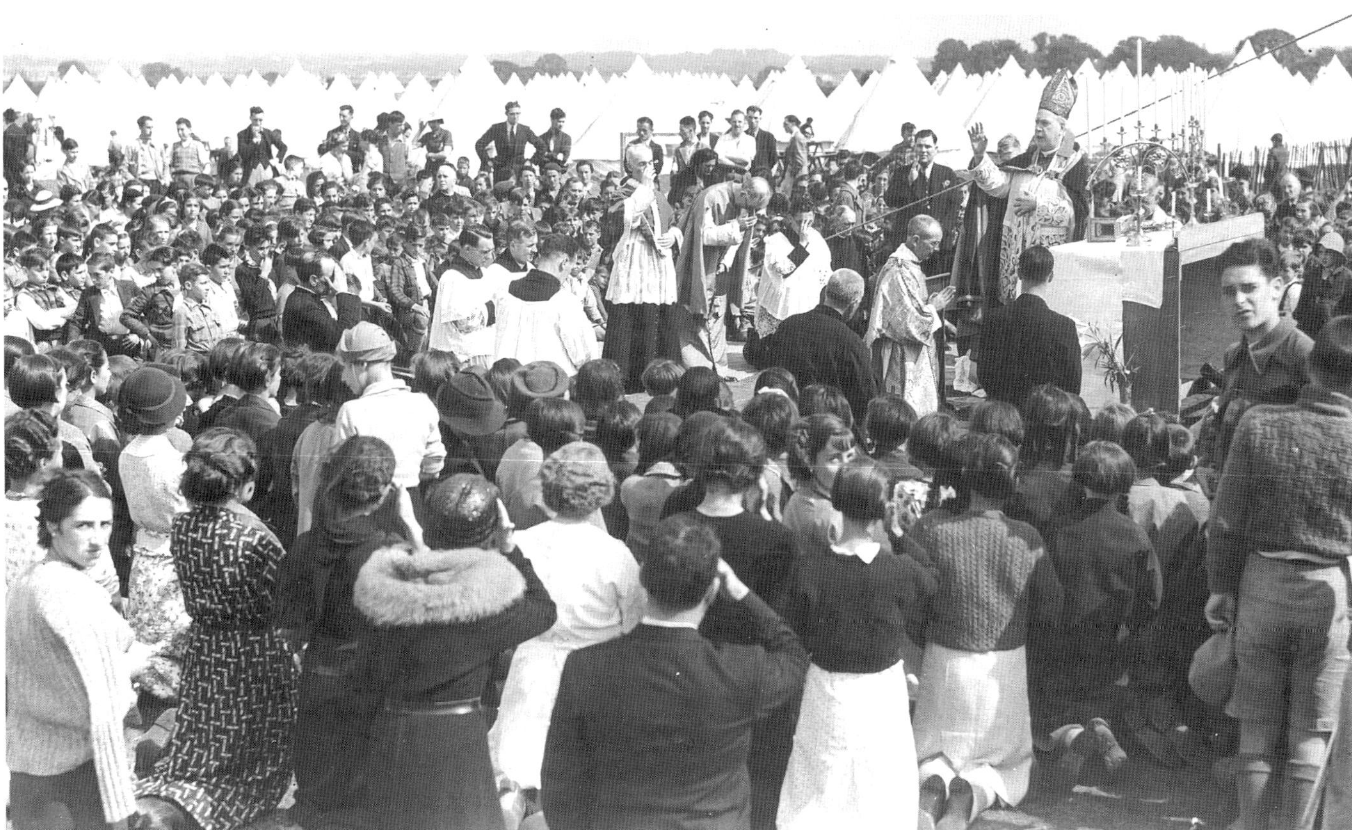

The scene at Stoneham Camp, Eastleigh, Hampshire in June 1937 as Bishop William Cotter of Portsmouth gives Benediction to young Basque refugees. The camp was established under the auspices of the Basque Children's Committee in 1937 to care for the children of Basque refugees from the Spanish Civil War. In May 1937 over 3,000 refugee children arrived in Britain on the ship Habana and were taken to the North Stoneham Camp, which had been swiftly erected by volunteers to receive them. The camp was intended as a stop-gap measure and, following the dispersal of the children to host families, it closed down in September 1937.

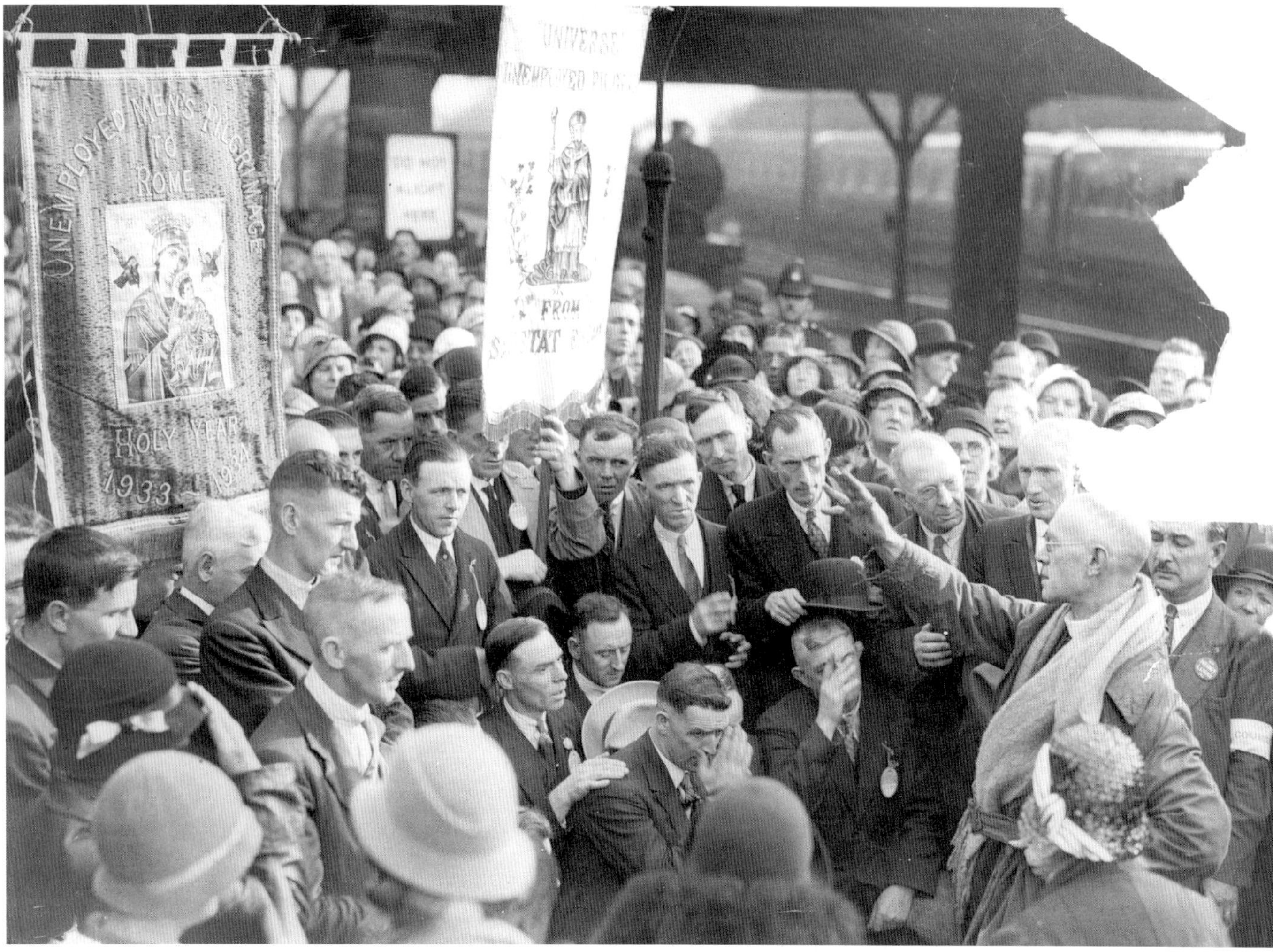

It was such a shame that this fantastically detailed study was in such a poor condition. It took several days to piece the flaking fragments together, and electronically restore the image to this level. In the early 1930s *The Universe* organised a series of pilgrimages to Rome and Lourdes for unemployed men from the UK and Ireland. Wearing a stole over a muffler and a much-worn trench coat, The Jesuit writer Fr. C.C. Martindale blesses the pilgrimage banners on the platform in Victoria station. The Irish contingent's banner is on the right. The driver and fireman of the pilgrimage train were among the spectators at the ceremony.

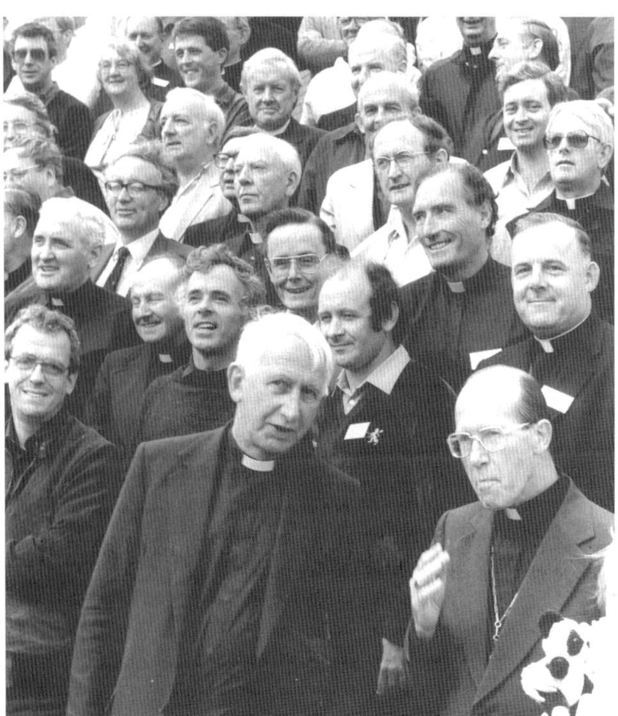

Cardinal Hume and Bishop Worlock in relaxed mood at the 1984 National Conference of Priests' conference.

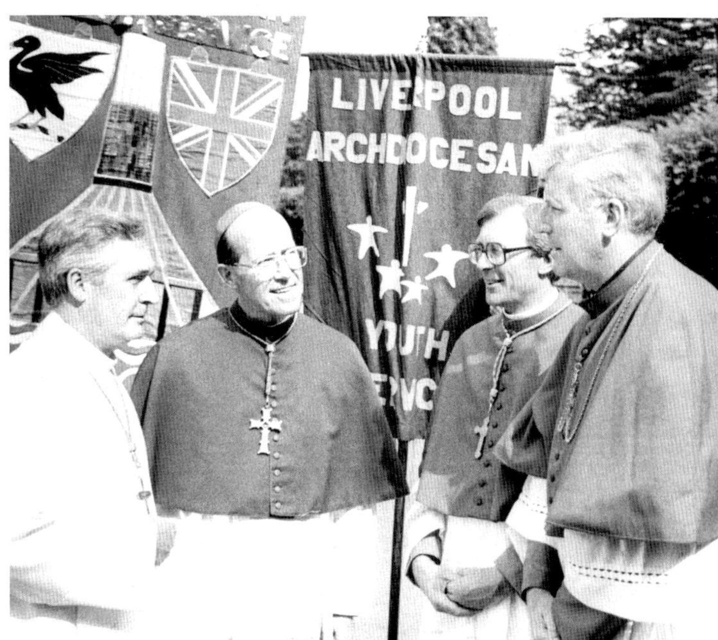

Archbishop Worlock enjoys a conversation during the December 1984 Liverpool Archdiocesan Youth Service with (left to right) Archbishop Thomas Winning of Glasgow, Bishop John Rawsthorne (then Auxilliary Bishop in Liverpool, now Bishop of Hallam) and Bishop (later Cardinal) Cormac Murphy O'Connor of Arundel and Brighton.

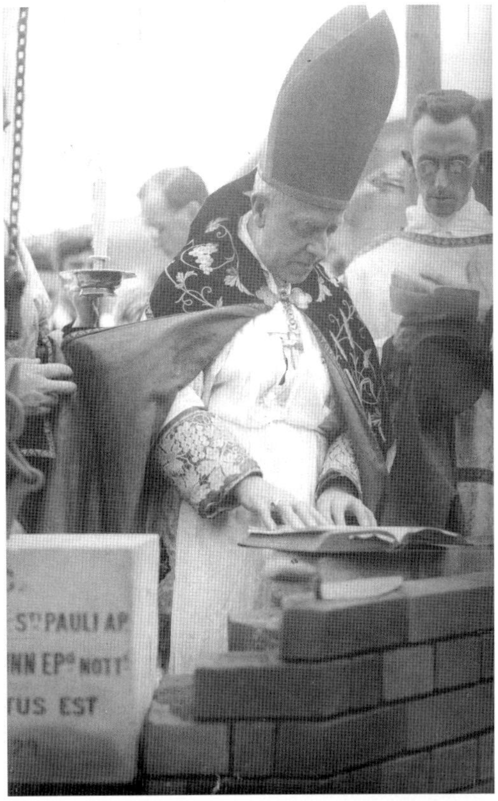

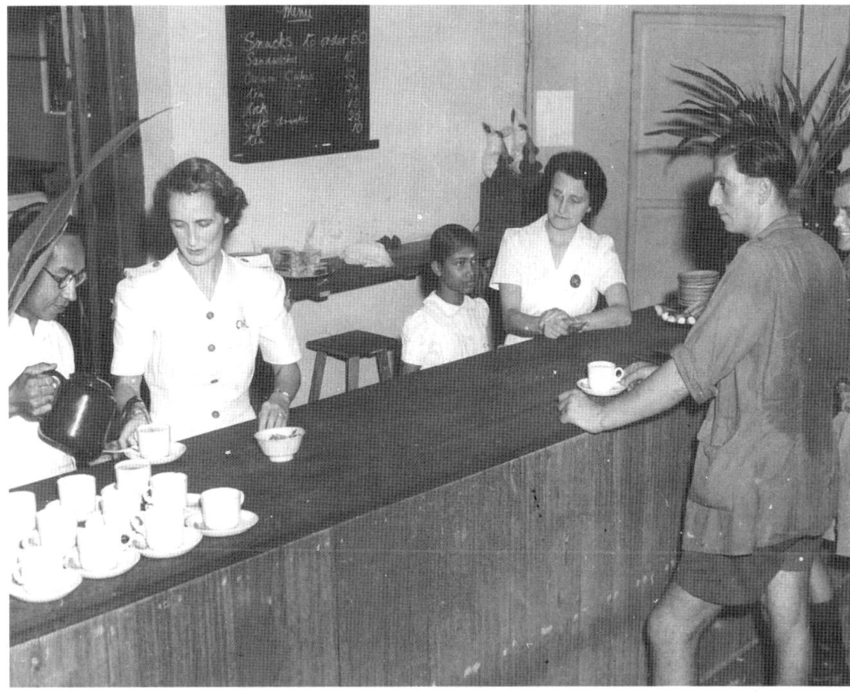

(Left) The bishop of Nottingham, Dr. Thomas Dunn, at the stone-laying ceremony in August 1929 to commence the building of a church dedicated to St. Paul, at Radford, Nottingham. (Above) Teatime at the Catholic Women's League canteen, Singapore in October 1946.

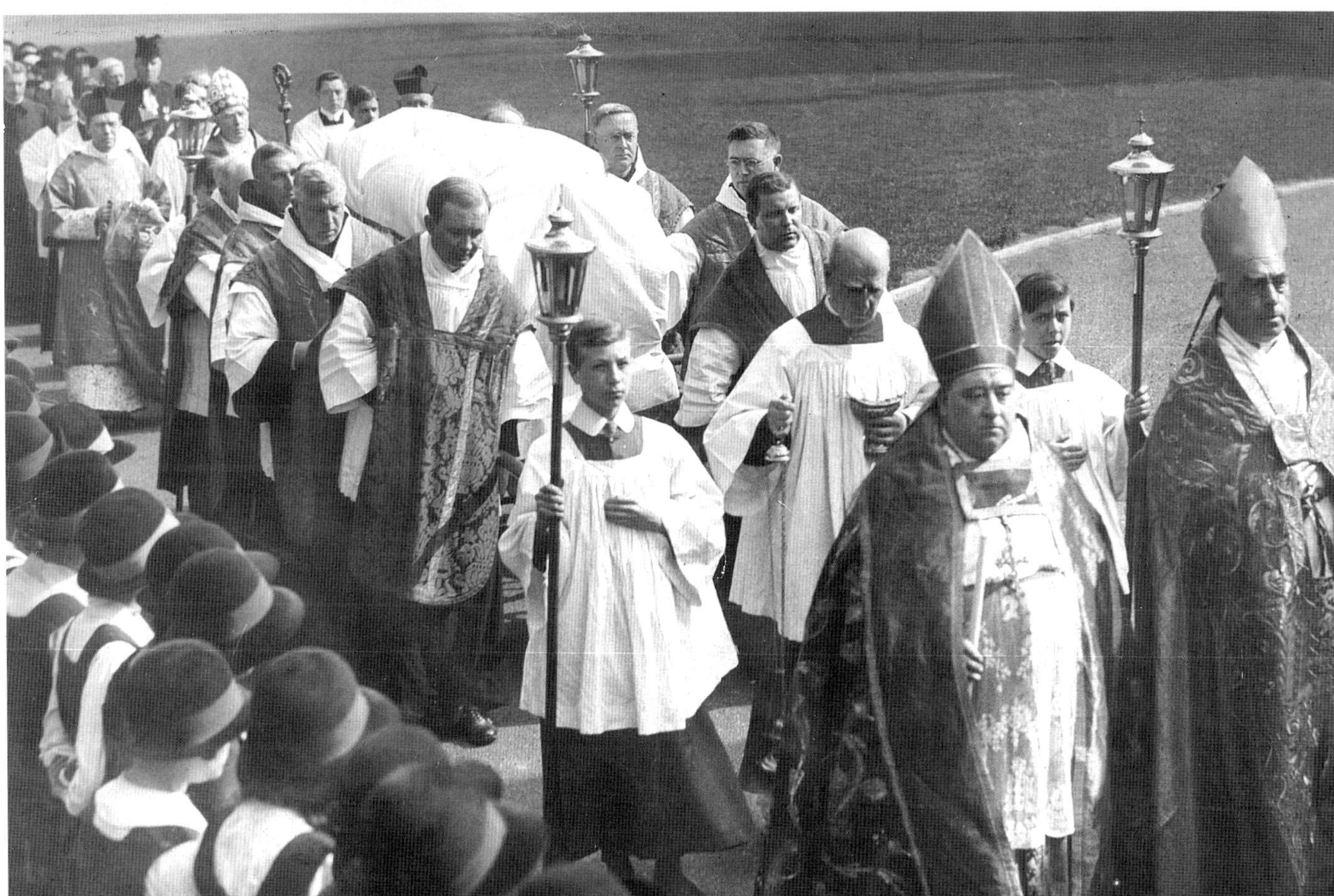

The scene outside Westminster Cathedral in May 1930, as Father (later Saint) John Southworth's body was taken there for reburial. Southworth was a member of the Southworth family of Samlesbury Hall, Blackburn, he was ordained priest at the English College, Douai, and was sent on the mission, 13th October, 1619. He was arrested and condemned to death in Lancashire in 1627, and imprisoned first in Lancaster Castle, and afterwards in the Clink, London. In 1636 he had been released and was living at Clerkenwell, but frequently visited the plague-stricken dwellings of Westminster to convert the dying. He was arrested several times and, after his final apprehension, he was tried at the Old Bailey, and as he insisted on pleading "guilty" to being a priest. He was condemned, and died on the gallows at Tyburn, on 28th June 1854. His remains passed to the Duke of Norfolk's family, who had them sent to the English College at Douai. They were hidden during the French Revolution, and were thought to have been lost, but they were dramatically rediscovered in 1927, and brought back to England, to be enshrined in Westminster. In 1970, John Southworth was canonised by Pope Paul VI among the Forty Martyrs of England and Wales, whose joint feast day is kept on 25th October.

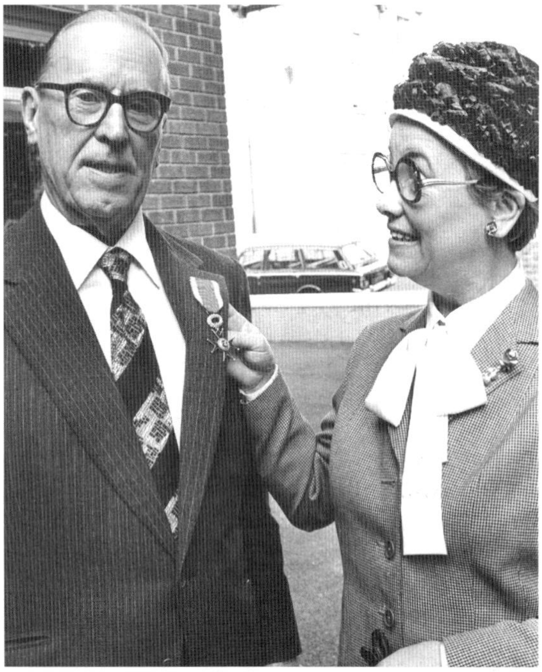

On Christmas Day 1946, Mrs. Jane Hodge died in a Cardiff nursing home. Her son, Julian, never forgot the loving care she was given there by the Sisters of the Sacred Hearts of Jesus and Mary.

Thirty two years later her son, by then the multi-millionaire banker and philanthropist Sir Julian Hodge, said thank-you by contributing £700,000 for a new home for the elderly, which was opened in October 1978 in Conwy Road, Cardiff by the speaker of the House of Commons, Mr. George Thomas.

The Jane Hodge Home, which included 30 beds for chronically ill and elderly patients, was to be run by the nuns.

Archbishop Murphy of Cardiff, after blessing the new home, installed Sir Julian as a Knight of St. Gregory.

Sir Julian Hodge was a London-born entrepreneur and banker who lived in Wales for most of his life, from the age of five. He formed the Bank of Wales, and later the Julian Hodge Bank in Cardiff.

As the son of a plumber, he came from humble beginnings. At the age of five he moved to Pontllanfraith, Wales. He left school at age 13 but his mother encouraged him to read classic novels and recite poetry to further his education. His first job was as an assistant in a chemist's shop. He joined the Great Western Railway as a junior clerk in 1920 and studied accountancy in his spare time, qualifying as a corporate accountant in 1930. He went into business for himself in the early 1930s.

He was well known as a philanthropist, using much of his fortune for charity work. In the late 1990s he helped fund the "Just Say No" campaign against devolution ahead of a referendum for the Welsh assembly, and the Euro-Know campaign opposed to the introduction of the Euro in the UK.

In the 2004 *Sunday Times* rich list his fortune was estimated at £48 million, making him the 18th richest person in Wales.

He died peacefully at his home on the island of Jersey, just three months short of his 100th birthday.

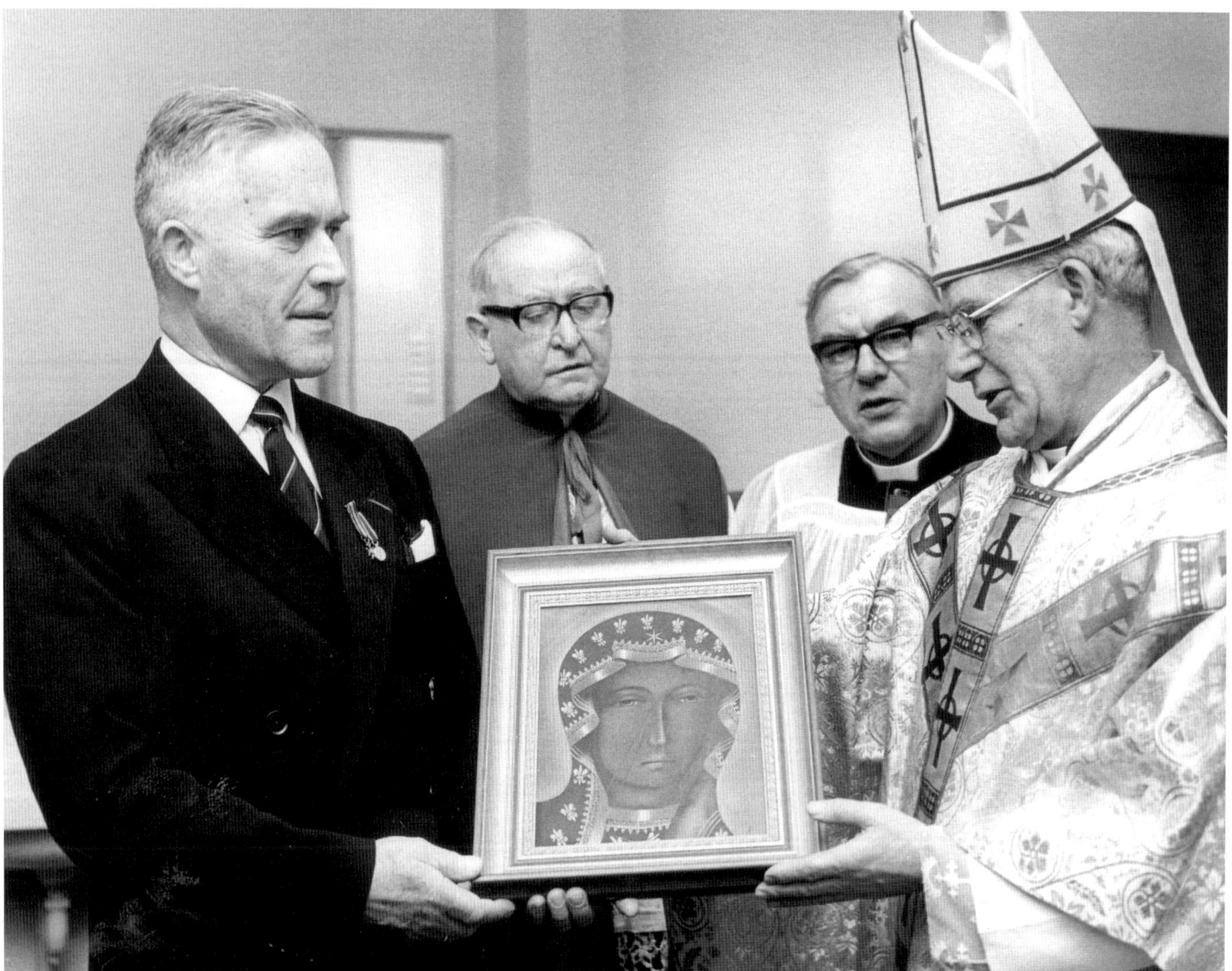

While a naval chaplain, Bishop Holland of Salford gave the last rites to men of the Polish cruiser Dragon, torpedoed and beached west of Le Havre during the invasion of Europe in 1944. The cruiser's commander promised to give Fr. Holland a painting of Our Lady of Czestochowa, known as the Black Madonna, which hung on board, but in the turmoil of invasion it was missing. On Sunday 8th February 1970, the Manchester Polish Naval Association redeemed that promise. Lieut. Commander Lesisz, one of the survivors from the Dragon, organised the presentation of a facsimile painting from the shrine at Czestochowa of the famous picture, in the Polish church of Our Lady of Divine Mercy in Moss Side. Pictured at the presentation are (from left) Capt. Bogdan Wronski, Mgr. Wladyslaw Staniszewski, Mgr. Jan Bas (parish priest) and Bishop Holland.

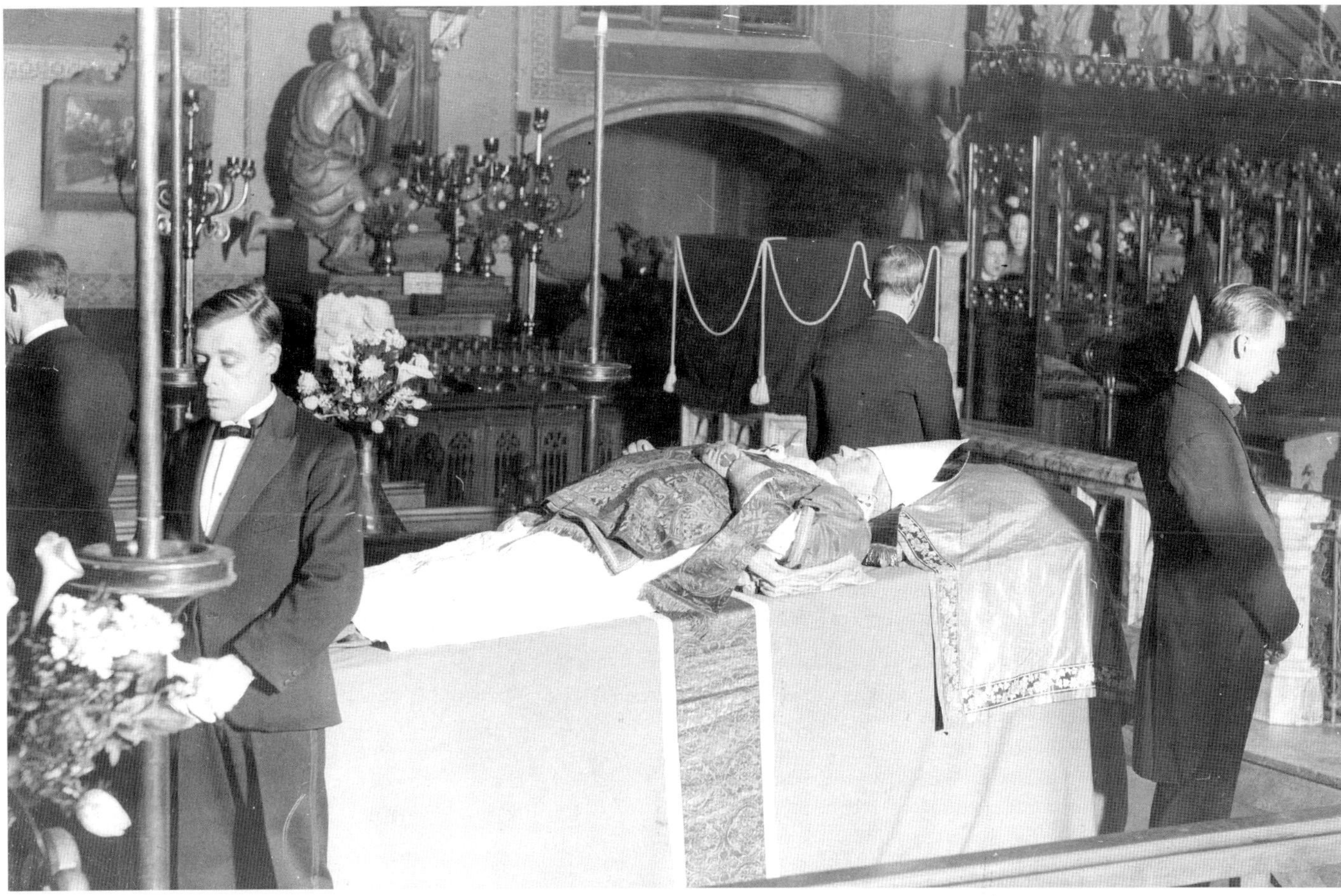

The body of the late Archbishop of Liverpool, Dr. Keating, pictured lying in state in St. Nicholas' Pro-Cathedral on 7th February 1928. From Friday night until Tuesday morning the body was watched continuously by a guard of Knights of St. Columba. They wore evening dress at night, and ordinary clothes during the day.

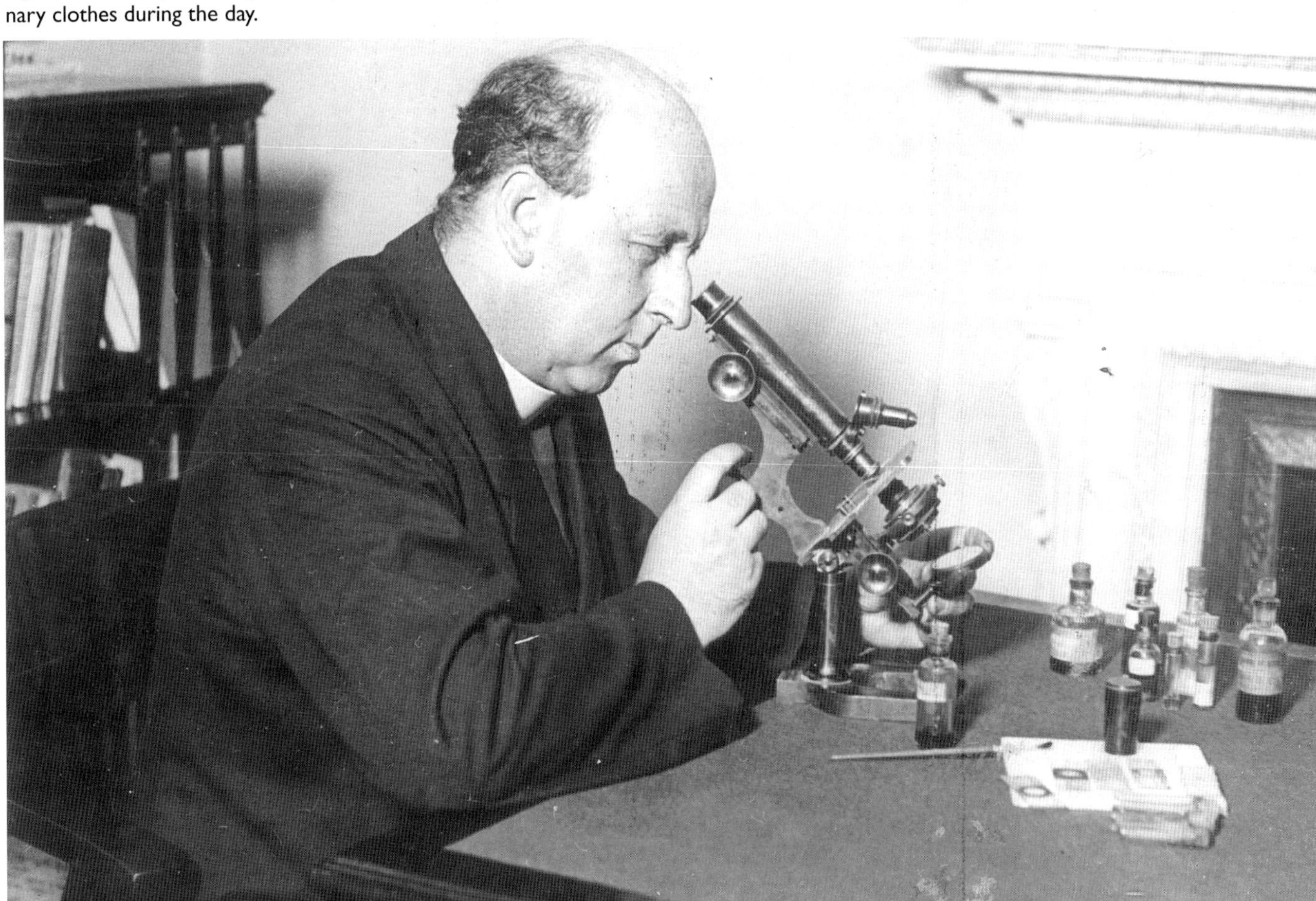

Father Philip de Ternant, author of *From an Old Priest's Diary*, one of the most popular series to have appeared in *The Universe* Catholic weekly, which first appeared in January 1928. Fr. De Ternant died in November 1943 at the RC Nursing Institute, Lambeth.

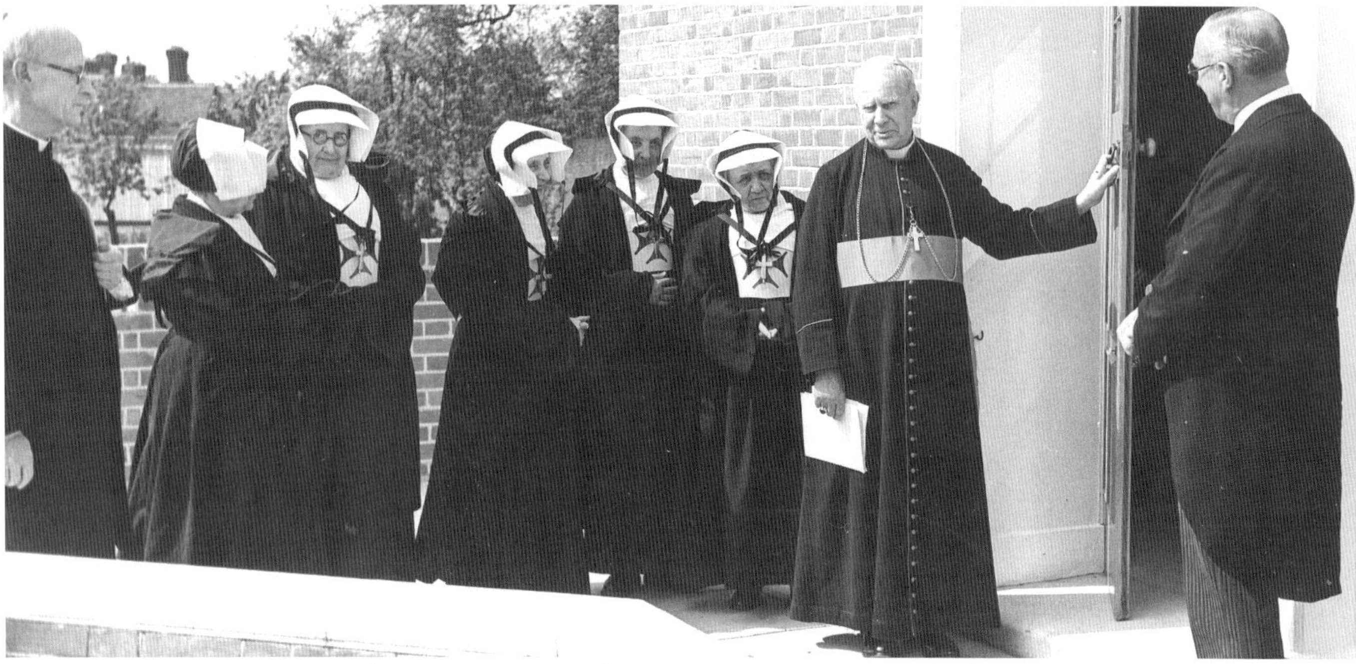

Archbishop Peter Emanuel Amigo of Southwark pictured at Bromley in June 1939 with some of the Sisters of the Holy Trinity whose convent he blessed and opened. Peter Amigo was born in Gibraltar in 1864. He studied at St Edmund's, Ware, and St. Thomas's, Hammersmith, and was ordained priest in 1888. He was professor at St. Edmund's from September 1888, to July 1892. He was assistant priest at Hammersmith from September 1892, to June 1896. He was afterwards at St Mary's and St Michael's, Commercial Road, East London, first as assistant priest, then as rector until April 1901, when he was then appointed rector of the mission at Walworth. He was consecrated Bishop of Southwark on 25th March 1904. Having received the personal title of Archbishop on 18th December 1937, he remained in control of the diocese until his death on 1st October 1949.

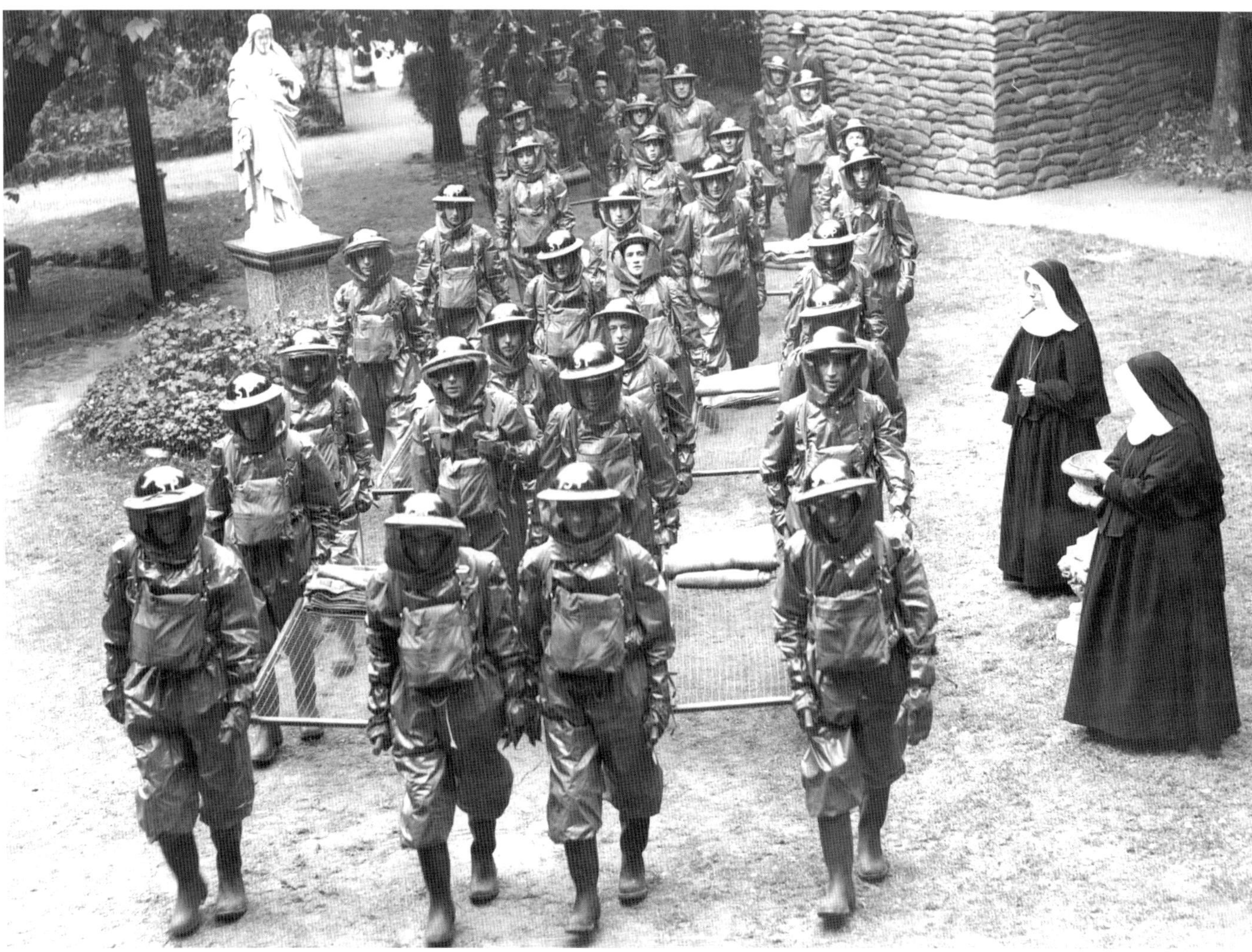

One of London's biggest ARP posts during the Second World War was this convent in London, which couldn't be identified for security reasons. The photographer for *The Universe* was given special access and took this study of stretcher parties on exercise in the convent garden, watched by two of the nuns who had taken a break from preparing meals for the men in October 1939.

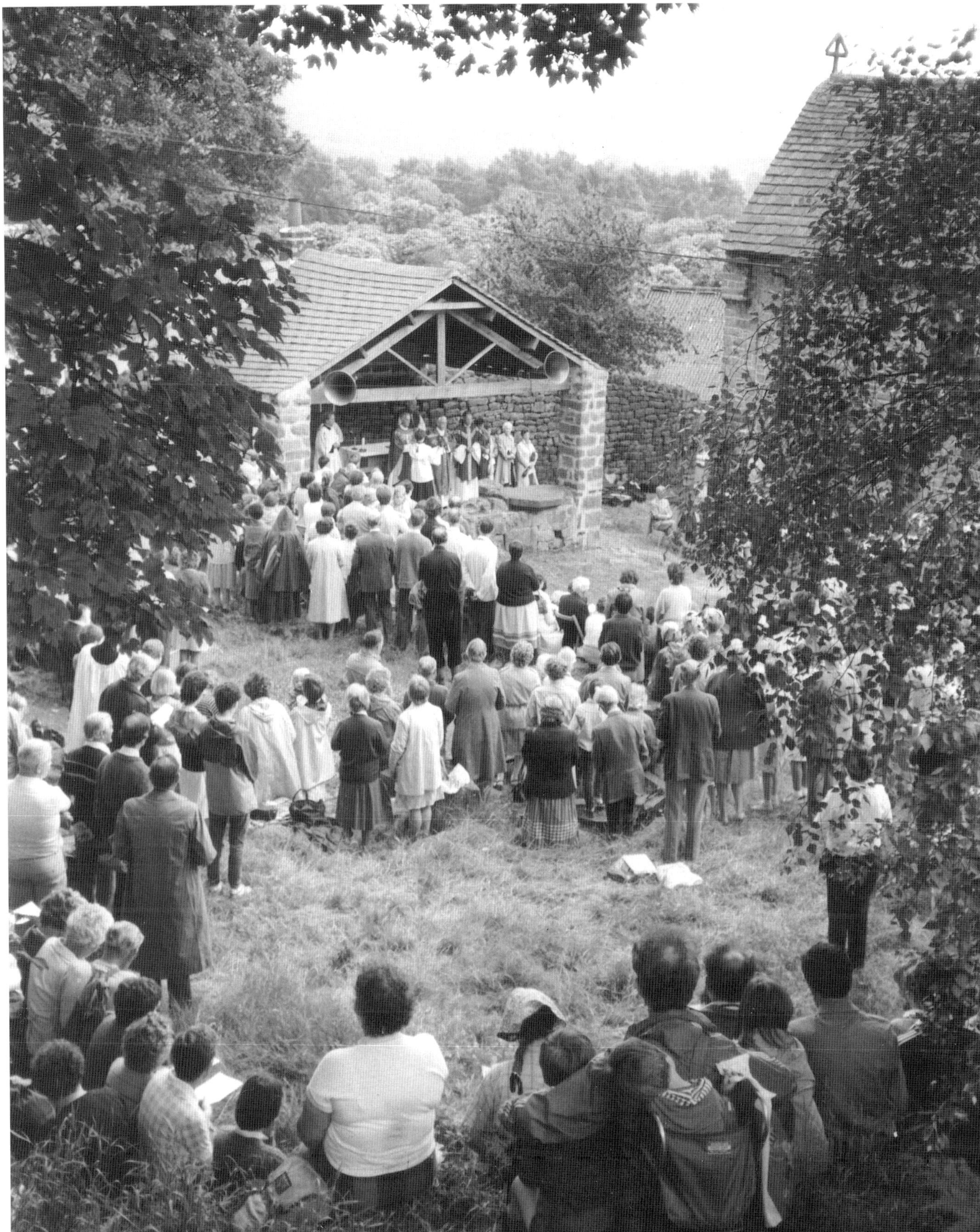

Pilgrims queue to receive Communion during the 1985 Middlesbrough Annual Diocesan pilgrimage to the shrine of Our Lady of Mount Grace, Ostmotherly, North Yorkshire. Mount Grace Priory, Ostmotherley, is one of only nine Carthusian priories founded in this country and is the best preserved. The 16th century Chapel of Our Lady of Mount Grace lies on a hill some 30 minutes walk above the priory. In 1665, the Franciscans took up residence and for a time young friars received their training in Osmotherley. The Franciscans ministered to the pilgrims. They remained there until 1832. The ruined chapel was bought in 1942 by the Roman Catholic diocese of Middlesbrough and by 1959 was restored. In 1969 the Franciscans returned and the buildings were expanded to cater for more pilgrims and pilgrimages. Later, the monks of Ampleforth Abbey took their place. It is also famous as the burial place of St. Margaret Clitherow of York. Margaret was literally crushed to death by having heavy stones placed on her chest because she would not admit to having sheltered Catholic priests. She died on Lady Day 1586 and it is believed that they carried her body for burial to Osmotherley, to the Chapel of Our Lady of Mount Grace.

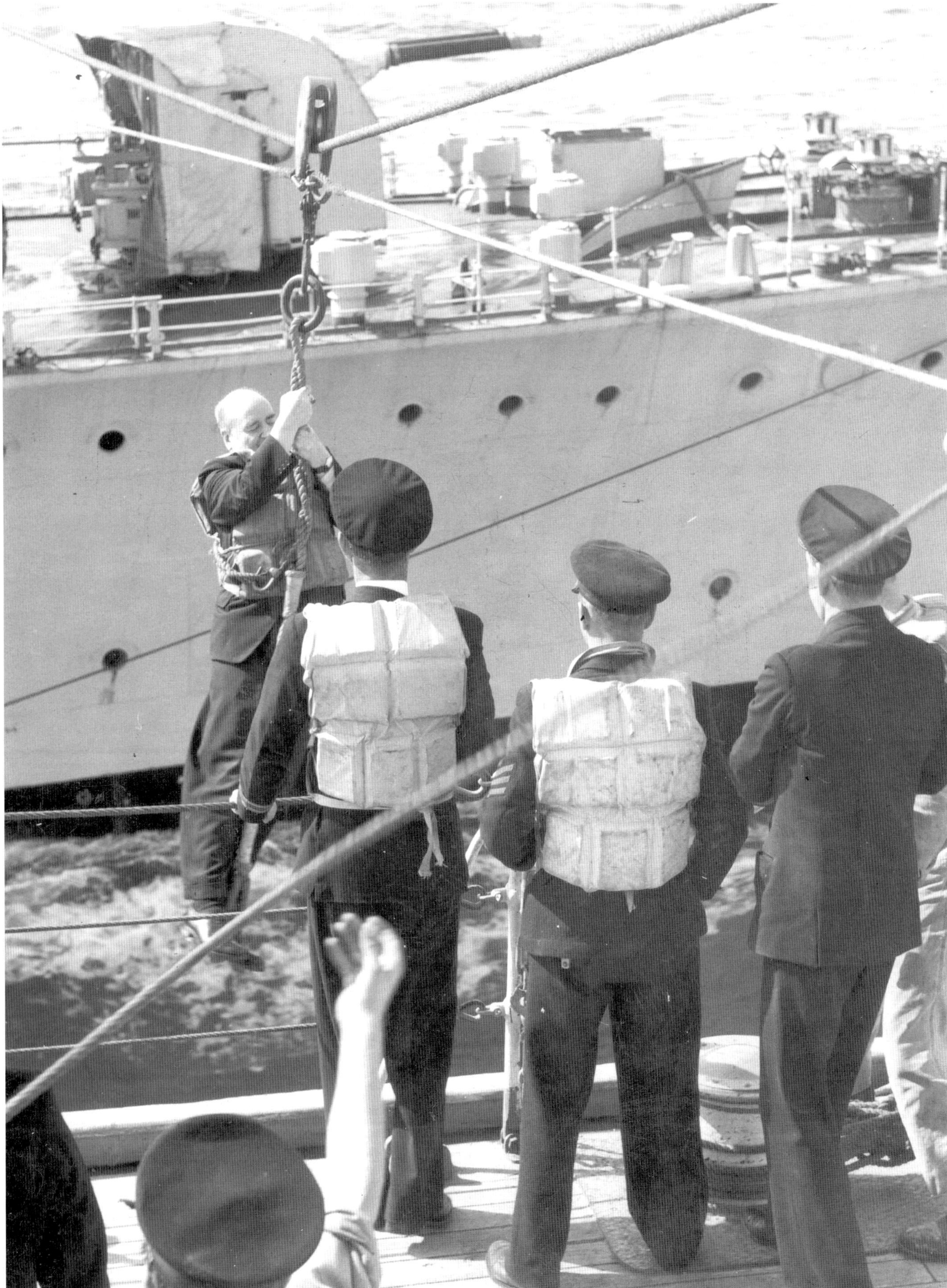

Archbishop Mathew, Bishop Ordinary to the Forces, is transferred by jackstay at sea from HMS Tyne, depot ship, to HMS Crossbow, destroyer, while on passage to Gibraltar in October 1954, where the Home Fleet was assembled during its Autumn cruise. The archbishop was in Gibralter for a fortnight, visiting Catholic officers and men of the three services, after which he travelled to Malta.

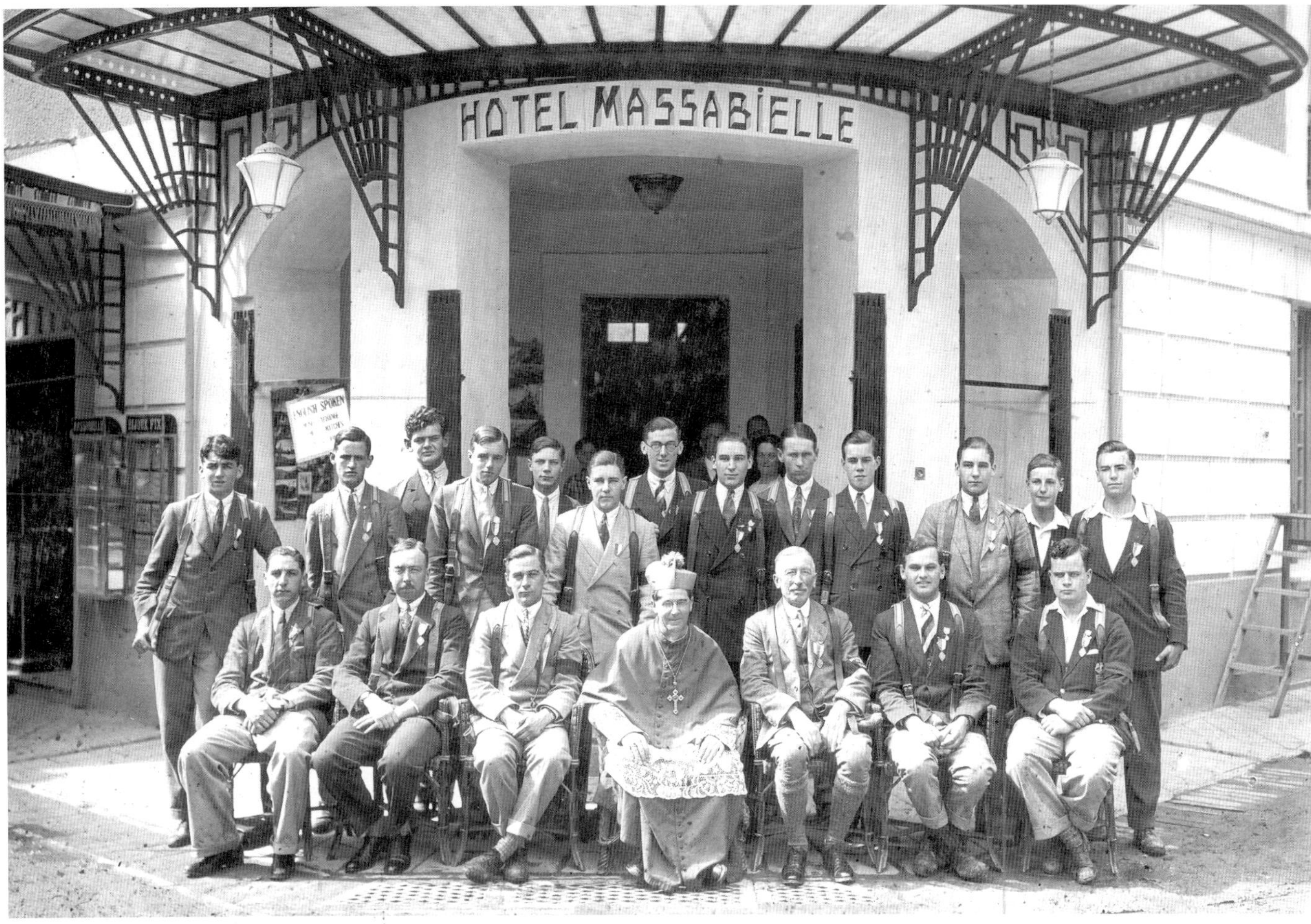

The Universe reported that pupils and old boys of Beaumont College "did sterling work" as brancardiers at Lourdes during the October 1927 Catholic Association Pilgrimage, which was led by the Bishop of Northampton, Bishop Dudley Charles Cary-Elwes. Pictured are: (back row from left) J. Tolhurst, J. Drummond, M. Hougalt, J. Strange, H. Noule, M. Cresswell, R. Wessel, T. Hilliman, D. Drummond, H. Strange, C. Hilleman, A. Romane, W. Jones. (Front row from left) G. Hood, Capt. Harrison, Capt. P.C. Leggetter MC (who was in charge of the party), Bishop of Northampton, Brig. Gen. G.H. Harrsion CB CMG, H. Houret, G. O'Connor.

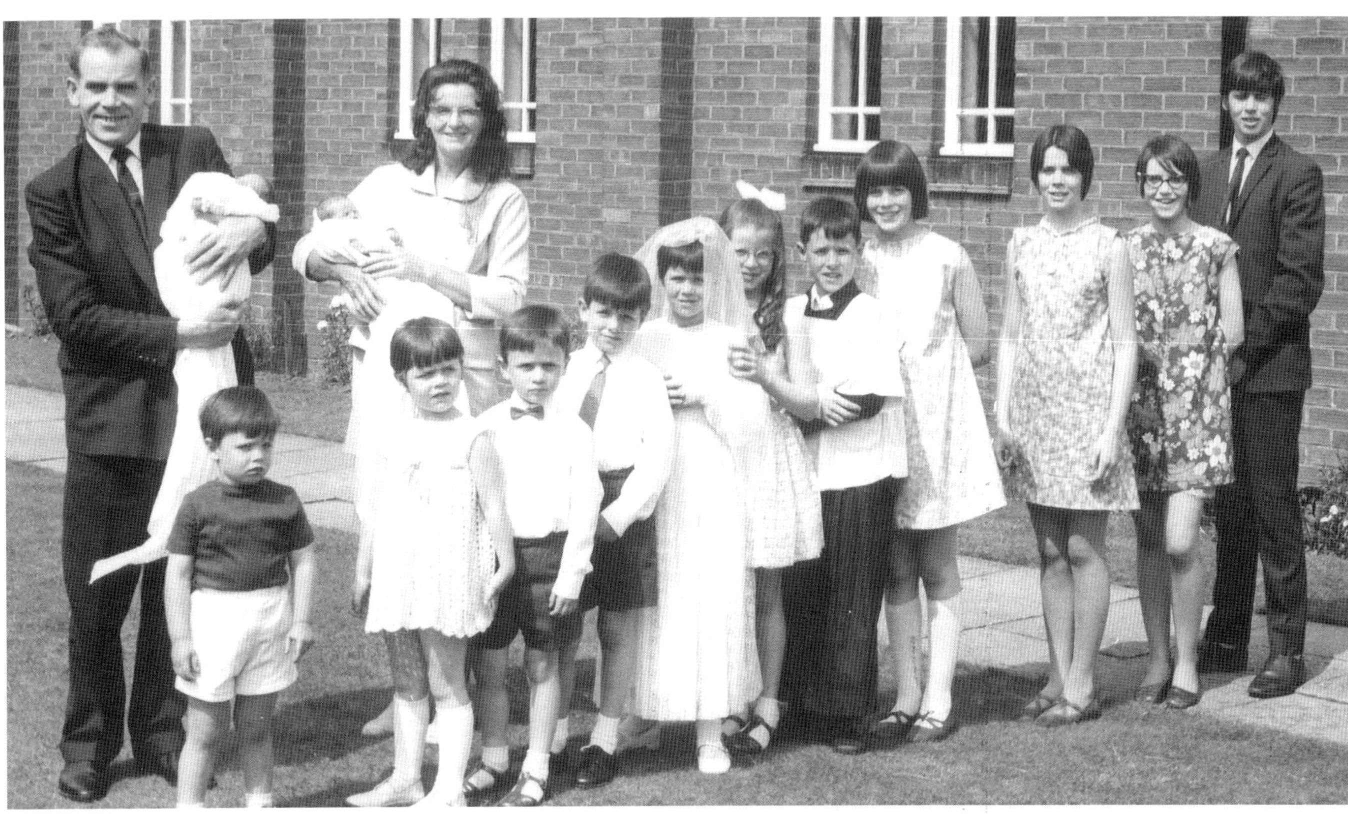

A proud day for Mr. and Mrs. Patrick Connole as they lined up with their 13 children after the christening of the latest addition to the family – five day old twins – at St. Mary Magdalene's, Maltby, Yorks in July 1969. Bishop Moverley, Auxiliary in Leeds, went to Maltby to officiate.

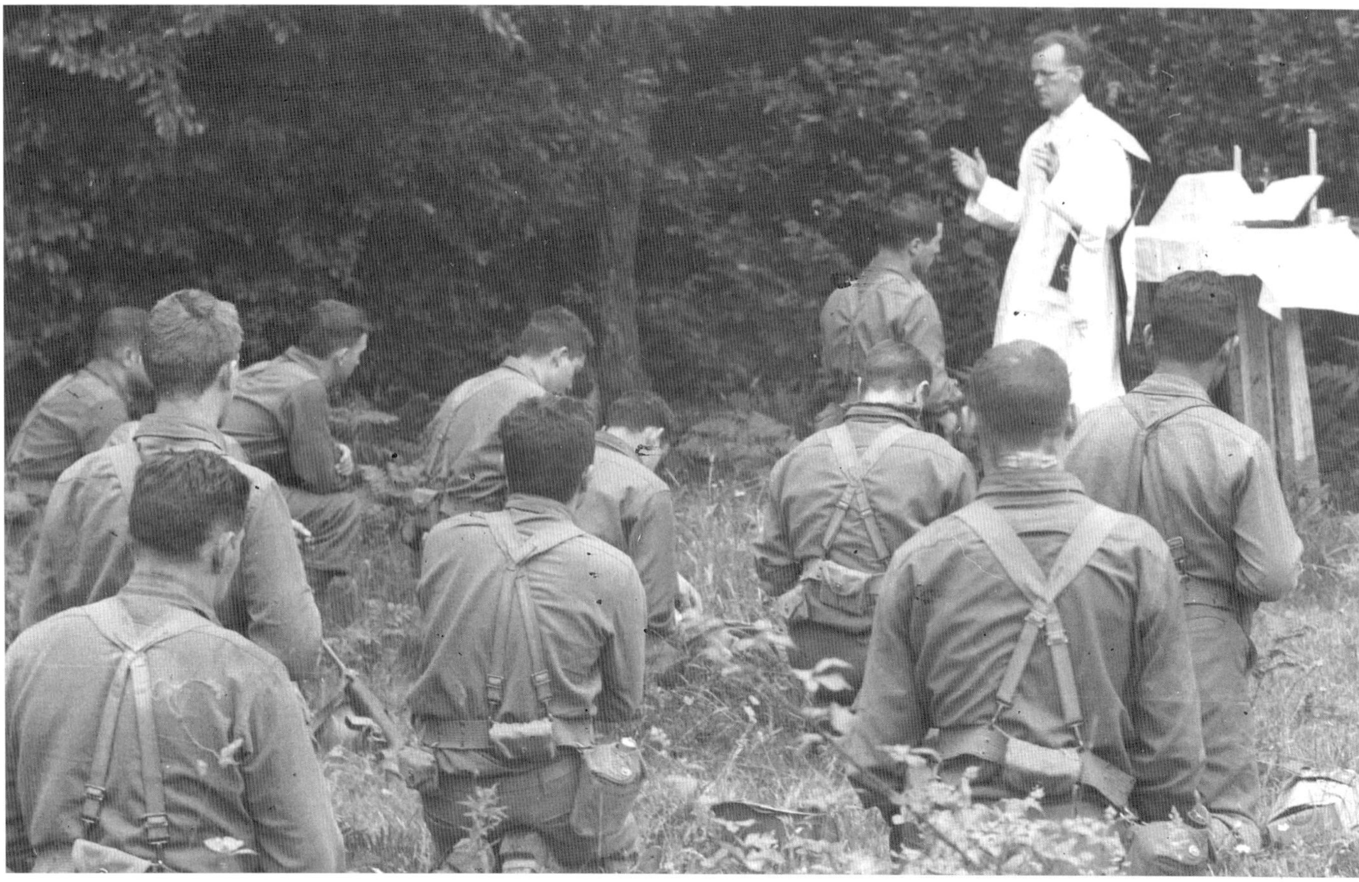

Snatching a brief spell during hard fighting on the Cherbourg Peninsula in July 1944, Allied soldiers hear Mass celebrated by their chaplain in the cover of trees just beyond the front line. *The Universe* pointed out that "most of the Catholics in ther British Army made their Confession and received Holy Communion before setting out to liberate occupied France."

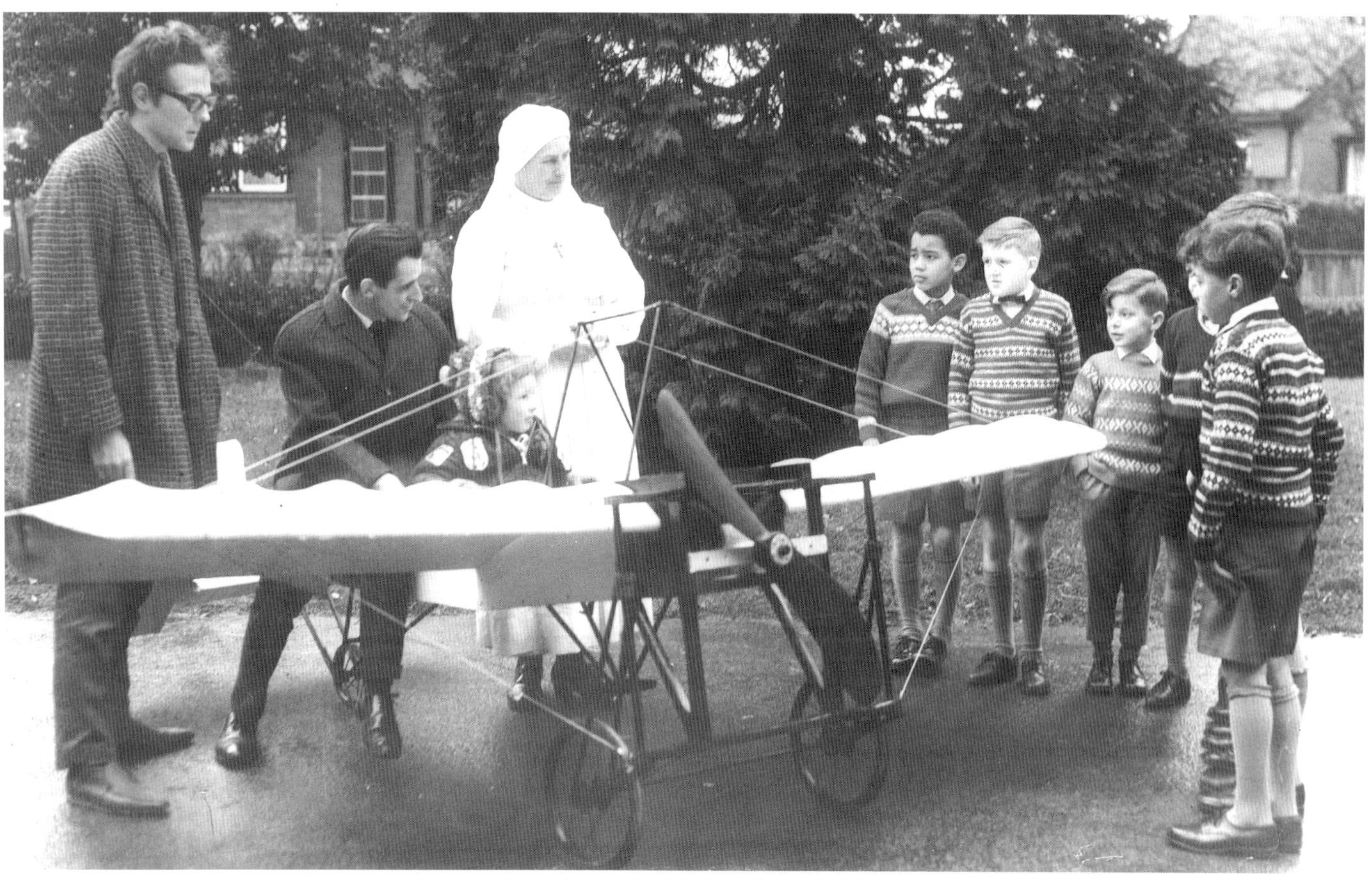

"Contact, chocks away!" Mother Teresa with some of her young charges at the Fr. Hudson Homes in Coleshill, near Birmingham watch as an intrepid six year old prepares to test a Bleriot model earoplane. Also pictured are two members of the Tudor Falcon Model Aero Club, of Sutton Coldfield, who made and presented the machine to the Home. It boasted a 10ft wingspan and the *Universe* reported that "it will taxi quite well – if the groundcrew are prepared to push!" The model was an exact replica of the Bleriot X1 monoplane which flew the English Channel in 1909.

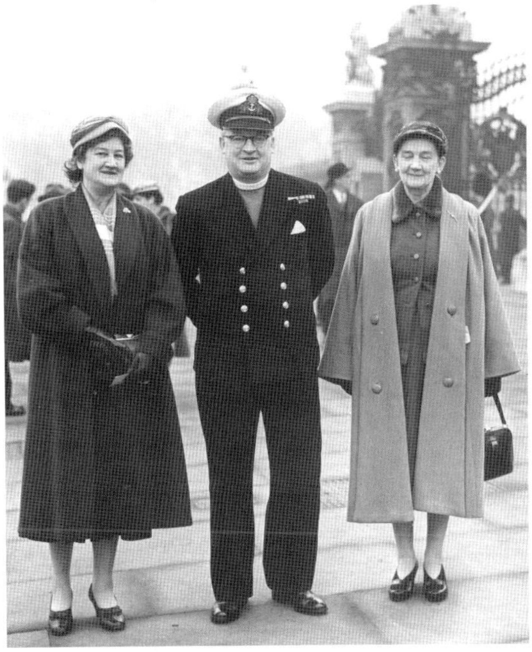

Mgr. William Shepherd, former Vicar General for the Navy and later parish priest of Our lady, St. Maws, Cornwall, leaves Buckingham Palace with his sisters in March 1957 after receiving the CBE.

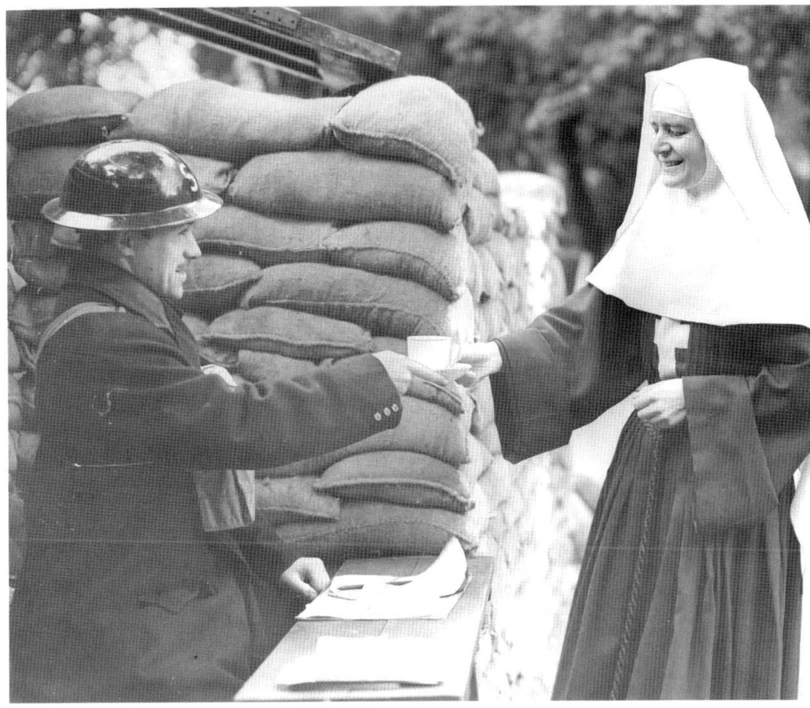

At an ARP post "somewhere in the Home Counties" in October 1939 a nun hands a welcome cup of tea to an air raid warden.

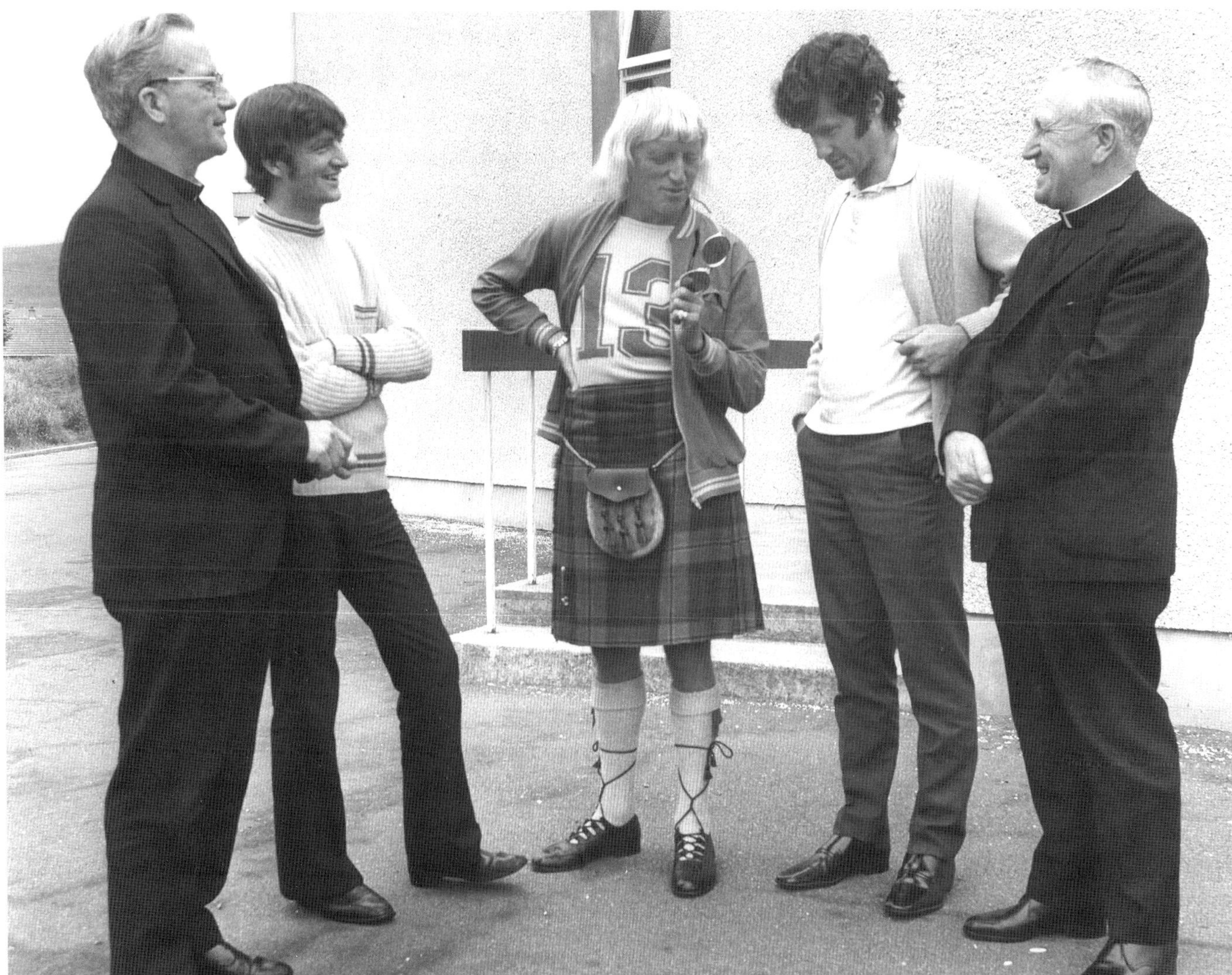

When disc jockey Jimmy Savile was in Fort William in August 1973 to take the role of Chieftain at the Lochaber Highland Games, he took time off for a very special occasion. Fr. Denis O'Connell, of St. Patrick's, Kilsyth, was joined by two deacons from the Kiltegan Fathers in a Mass for Mrs. Agnes Savile ('The Duchess'), Jimmy's beloved mother, who had died the previous year. Jimmy is pictured chatting after the service to Fr. O'Connell (left), Fr. Morrison, parish priest of Coal, and the two (un-named) deacons.

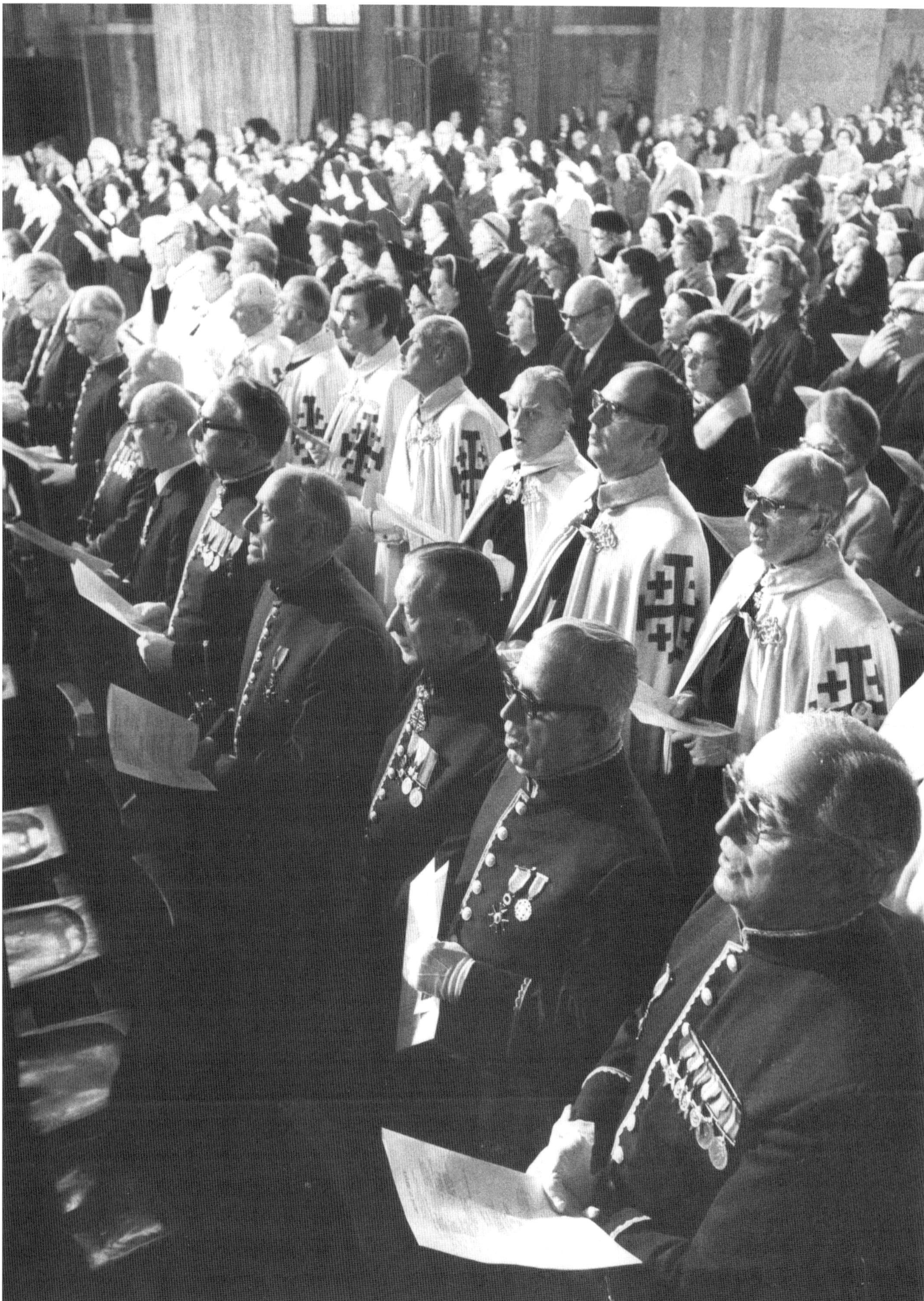

Papal Knights of St. Gregory and Knights of the Holy Sepulchre at the Requiem for Cardinal Heenan at Westminster Cathedral in November 1975.

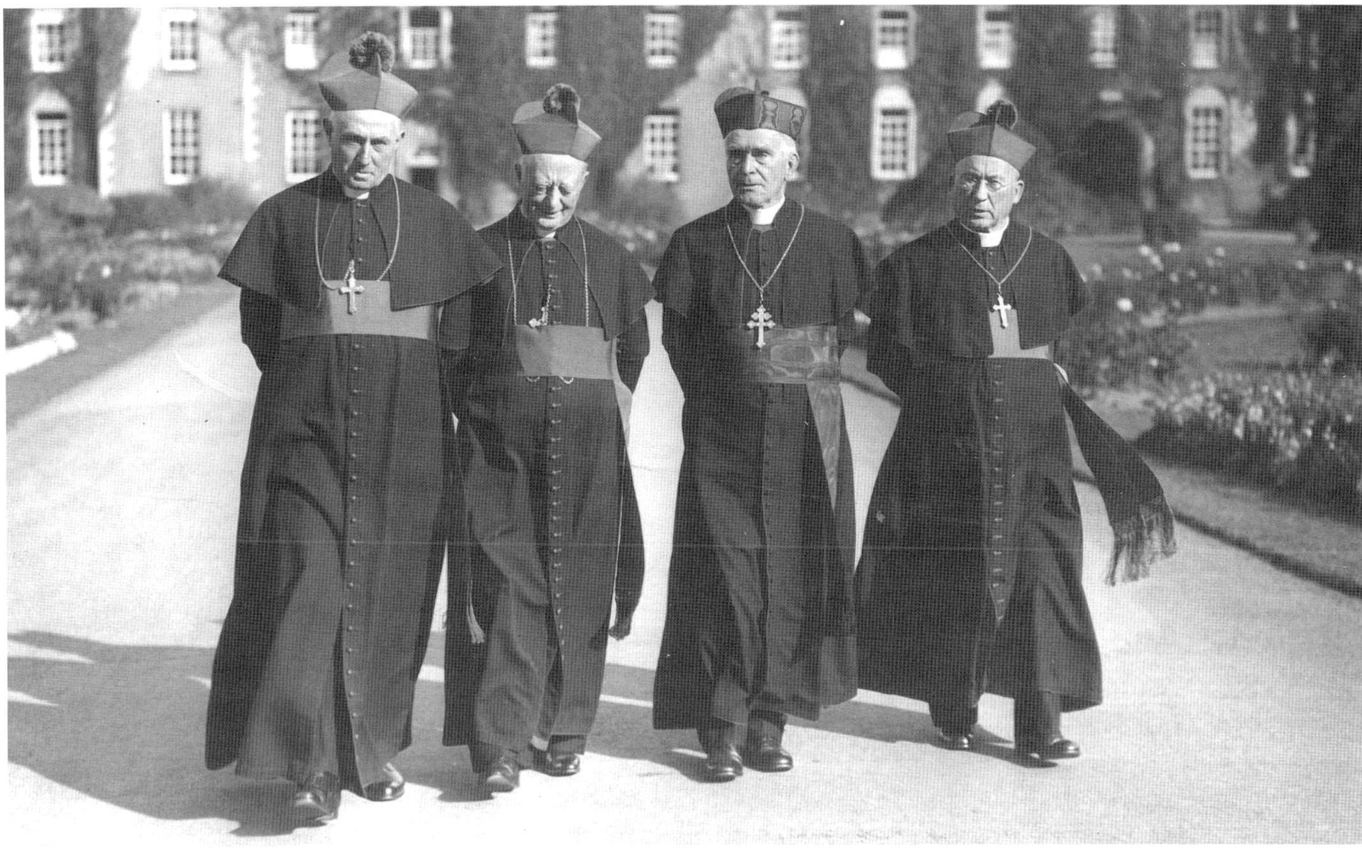

Cardinal McRory, second from right, pictured in the grounds of Maynooth College, Co. Kildare, with Dr. Mulvany (Bishop of Meath), Dr. Morrisroe (Achonry) and Dr. Roche (Bishop of Cloyne) before a meeting of the Irish bishops in October 1937.

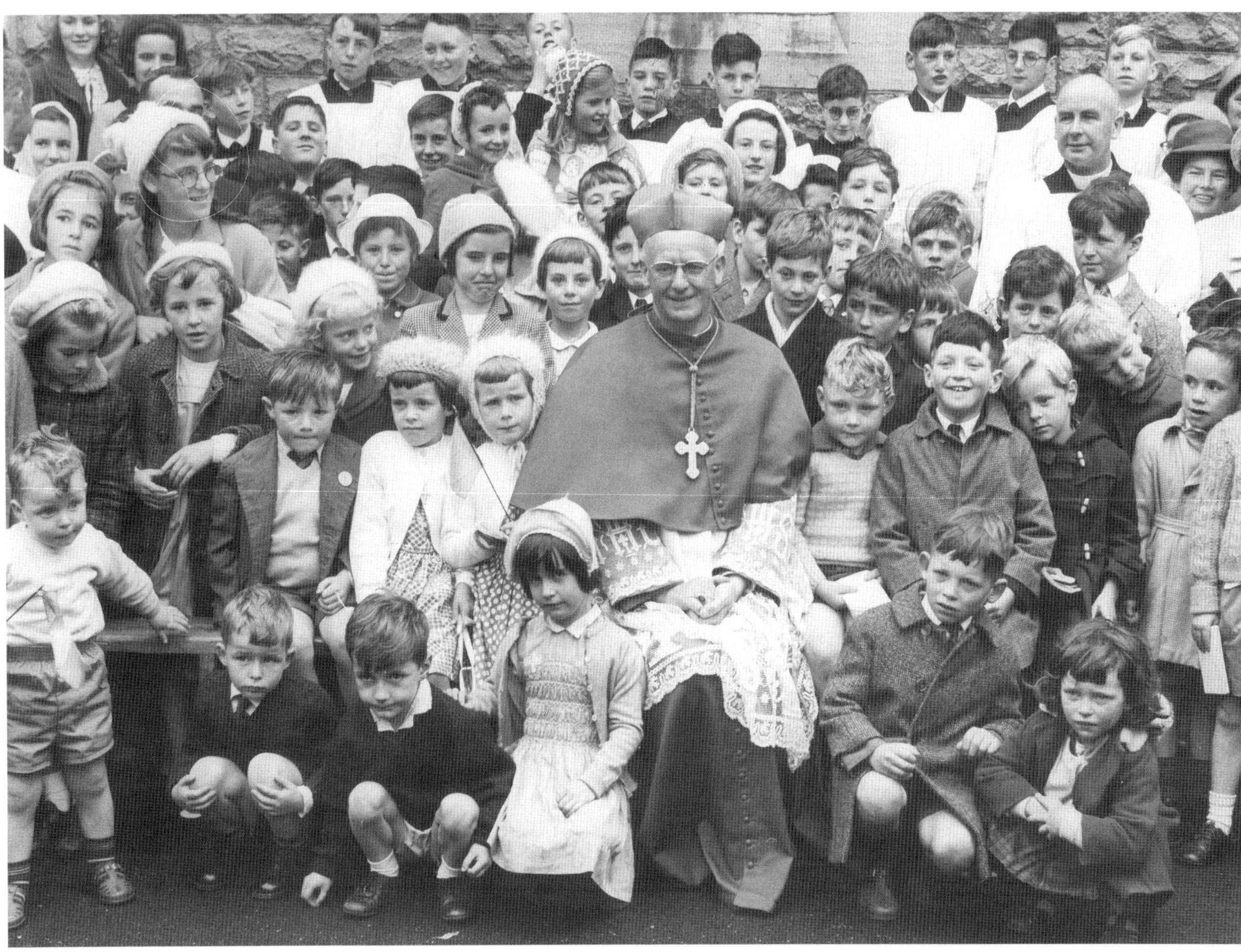

Cardinal John Carmel Heenan enjoys a relaxing moment with schoolchildren at Clareen, Co. Offaly in August 1965.

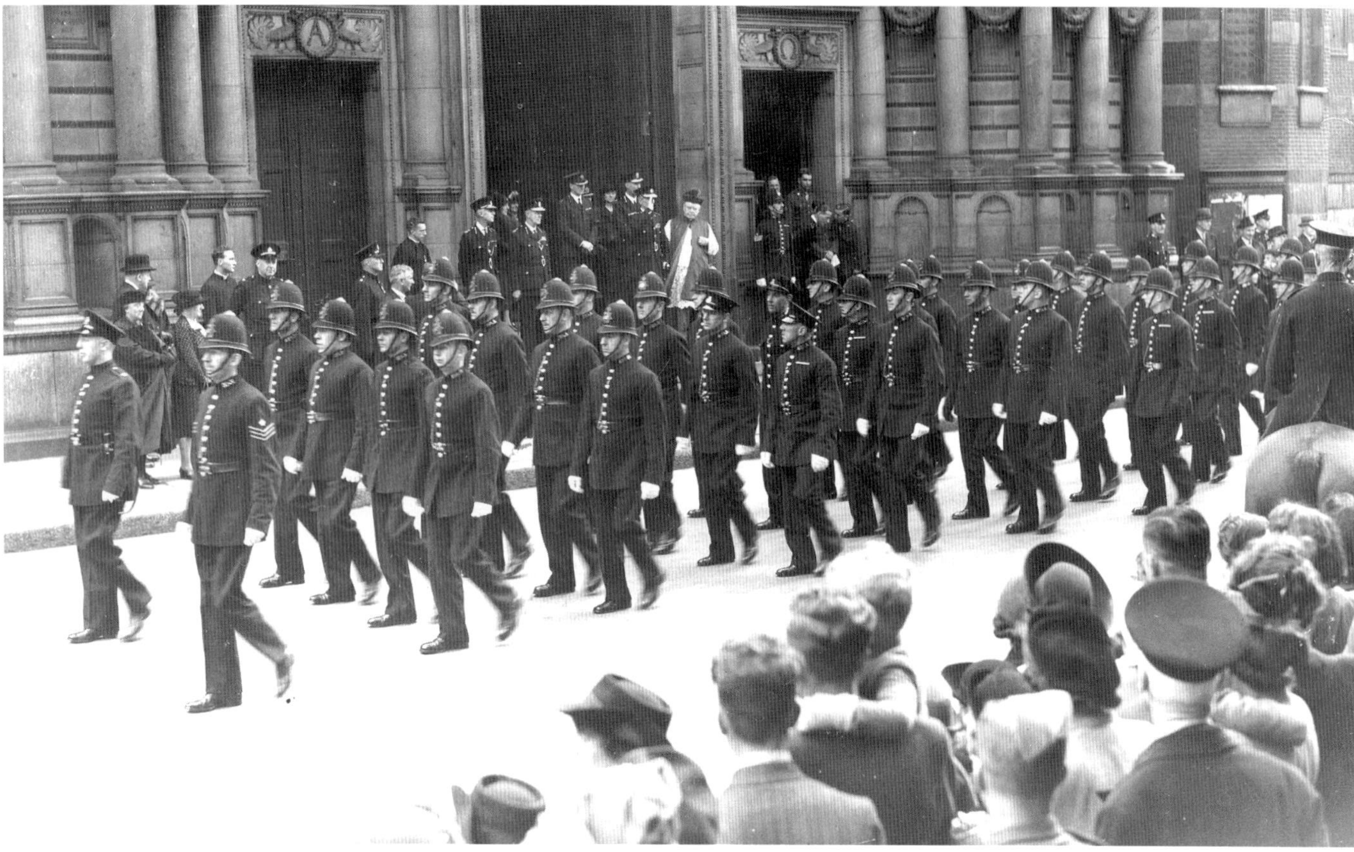

At the height of wartime, London Metropolitan and City police take time out to attend their annual Requiem Mass at Westminster Cathedral in October 1942 for deceased members, including those killed in air raids and other war activities. Over 600 policemen were present.

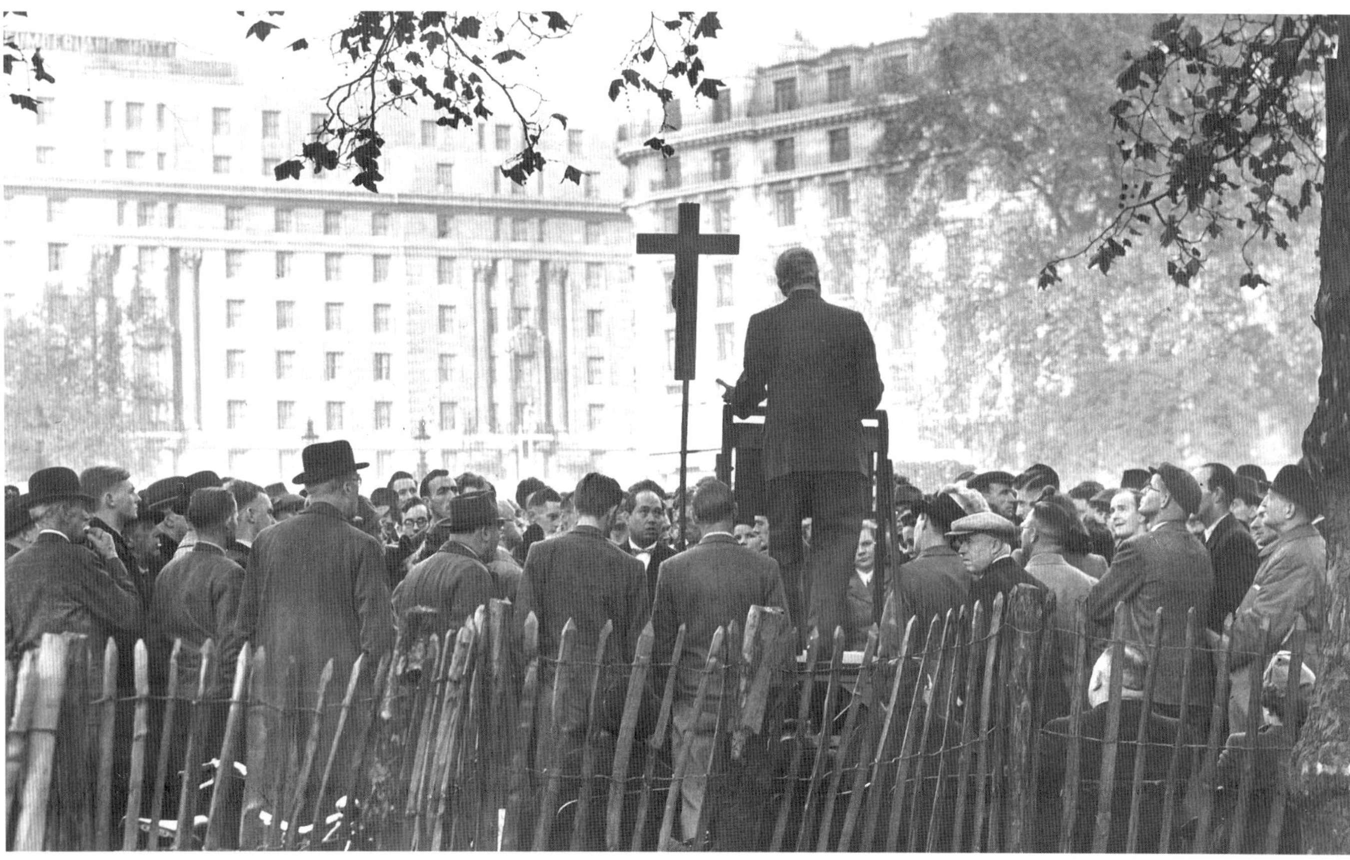

Frank Sheed was one of the most remarkable figures in 20th century English Catholicism, and was a central figure in the 'Catholic Intellectual Revival', an influential and loosely knit group of converts to the Faith, including authors such as G.K. Chesterton, Evelyn Waugh, Arnold Lunn, and Ronald Knox. An Australian of Irish descent, he graduated from Sydney University in Arts and Law, then moved in 1926, with his wife Maisie Ward, to London, where they founded the highly successful Catholic publishing company Sheed and Ward. A pioneer of the Catholic Evidence Guild, Frank could be found regularly taking to the CEG platform at Speakers' Corner in London's Hyde Park on a Sunday afternoon, answering questions on the Catholic faith and preaching to the crowds that gathered, as this rare photograph from the autumn of 1925 shows.

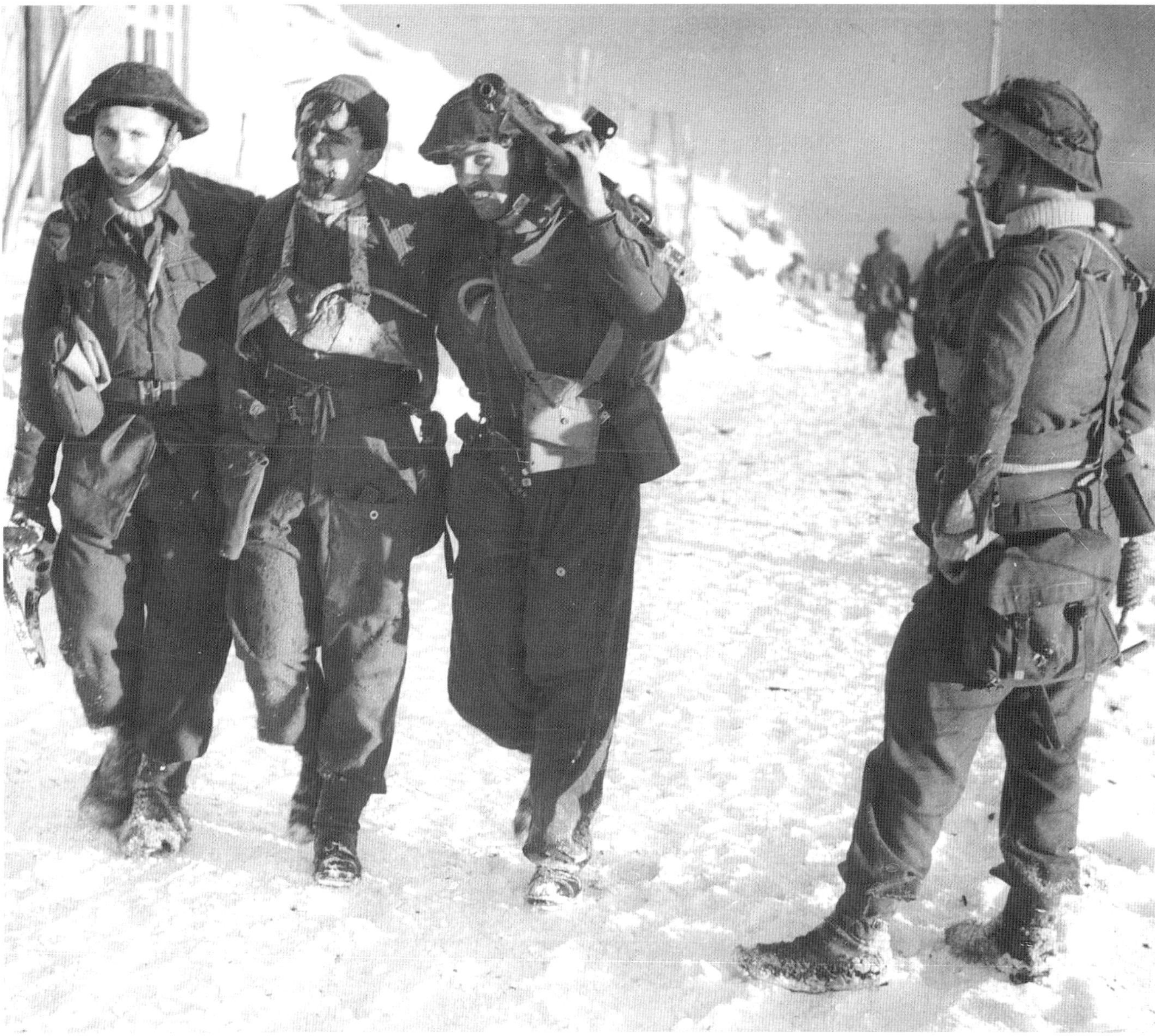

This remarkably rare photograph appeared in *The Universe* edition of 24th April 1942. It was taken during Operation Archery, a British Combined Operations raid during World War Two against German positions on Vaagso (Vågsøy), Norway on the 27*th* December 1941.

The raid was conducted by British Commandos of No.3 Commando, two troops (platoons) of No.2 Commando, a medical detachment of No.4 Commando, a demolition party from 101 Troop (canoe) of No.6 Commando and a dozen Norwegians from Norwegian Independent Company 1. The action was supported by Royal Navy gunfire, led by the cruiser HMS Kenya, and Royal Air Force bombers and fighter-bombers.

The dawn landing was preceded by a naval bombardment and objectives went according to plan, except in the town of Vaagso itself. Opposition there was much stiffer than expected as unknown to the British, a gebirgsjäger (mountain) unit of experienced troops from the Eastern Front was there on leave. Their experience in sniping and street fighting caused Vaagso to develop into a bitter house-to-house battle.

At around 14:00 the Commandos started their withdrawal having destroyed four factories, the fish-oil stores, ammunition and fuel stores, the telephone exchange and various military installations. Much of the town was in flames. The Naval assault force of one cruiser and four destroyers had meanwhile sunk 10 vessels, some found in the act of being scuttled to prevent capture.

Central to the operation was the destruction of fish-oil production and stores which the Germans used in the manufacture of high-explosives. Another intention was to cause the Germans to maintain and increase forces in Norway which otherwise might be employed on the Eastern Front. No Royal Navy ships were lost, but the Navy suffered four men killed and four wounded.

The Commandos sustained 17 killed and 53 wounded, and the RAF had 8 planes downed. The Commandos accounted for at least 120 enemy killed and returned with 98 prisoners and a complete copy of the German Naval Code.

The raid was enough to persuade Adolf Hitler to divert 30,000 troops to Norway, upgrade coastal and inland defences, and send the battleship Tirpitz, the battlecruisers (or light battleships) Gneisenau and Scharnhorst, the pocket battleship Lützow, and the heavy cruisers Admiral Hipper and Prinz Eugen to Norway - a major diversion of effort and forces that could have had significant impact elsewhere.

Hitler thought that the British might invade northern Norway to put pressure on Sweden and Finland.

The raid on Vaagso involved heavy street-to-street fighting, during which a 21 year old Catholic, Lieutenant Denis William Venebles Patrick O'Flaherty, was severely wounded. DWVP, as he was known, was an old boy of St. John's College, Southsea. Born in India, he was the only son of Lieut. and Mrs. O'Flaherty of St. Chad's Avenue, Portsmouth. He passed into the Royal Military Academy, Woolwich in 1938, and received his commission soon after the war began.

Our picture shows the young Royal Artillary Commando officer being rushed to an advanced dressing station to have his wounds tended to. Lieut. O'Flaherty was later awared the D.S.O. for his bravery during the raid. The leader of the raids, Brig. Haydon, also a Catholic, received a bar to his D.S.O.

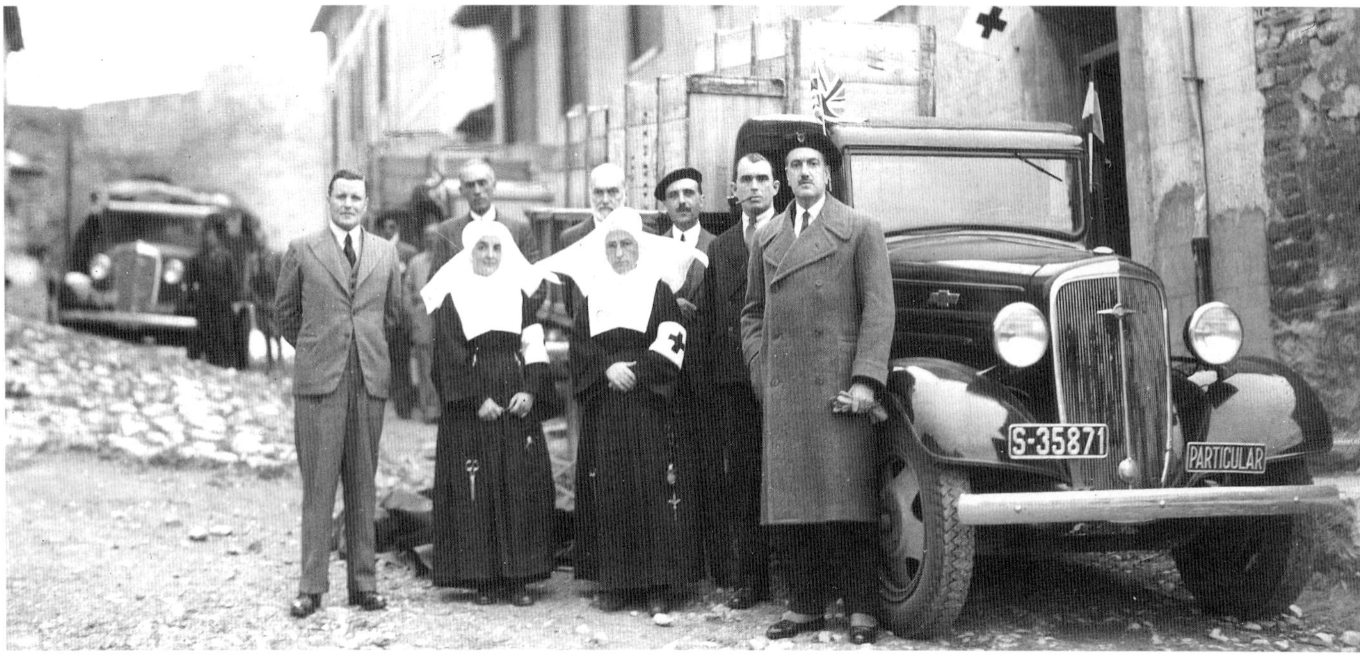

Throughout the Spanish Civil War, *The Universe* followed the rest of the Catholic Church in supporting the nationalist forces of General Franco. After calling for financial help from its readers, *The Universe* was able to send large amounts of aid to Spain, including food, clothing and several field ambulances. In October 1936 three "Universe" lorries containing medical supplies for "the anti-reds" as the national troops were called, arrived at the Burgos Red Cross headquarters. There to meet them were Catholic contacts in Spain, including nuns working as medics, and Count Vallellano (*far right*), Spanish Red Cross chief.

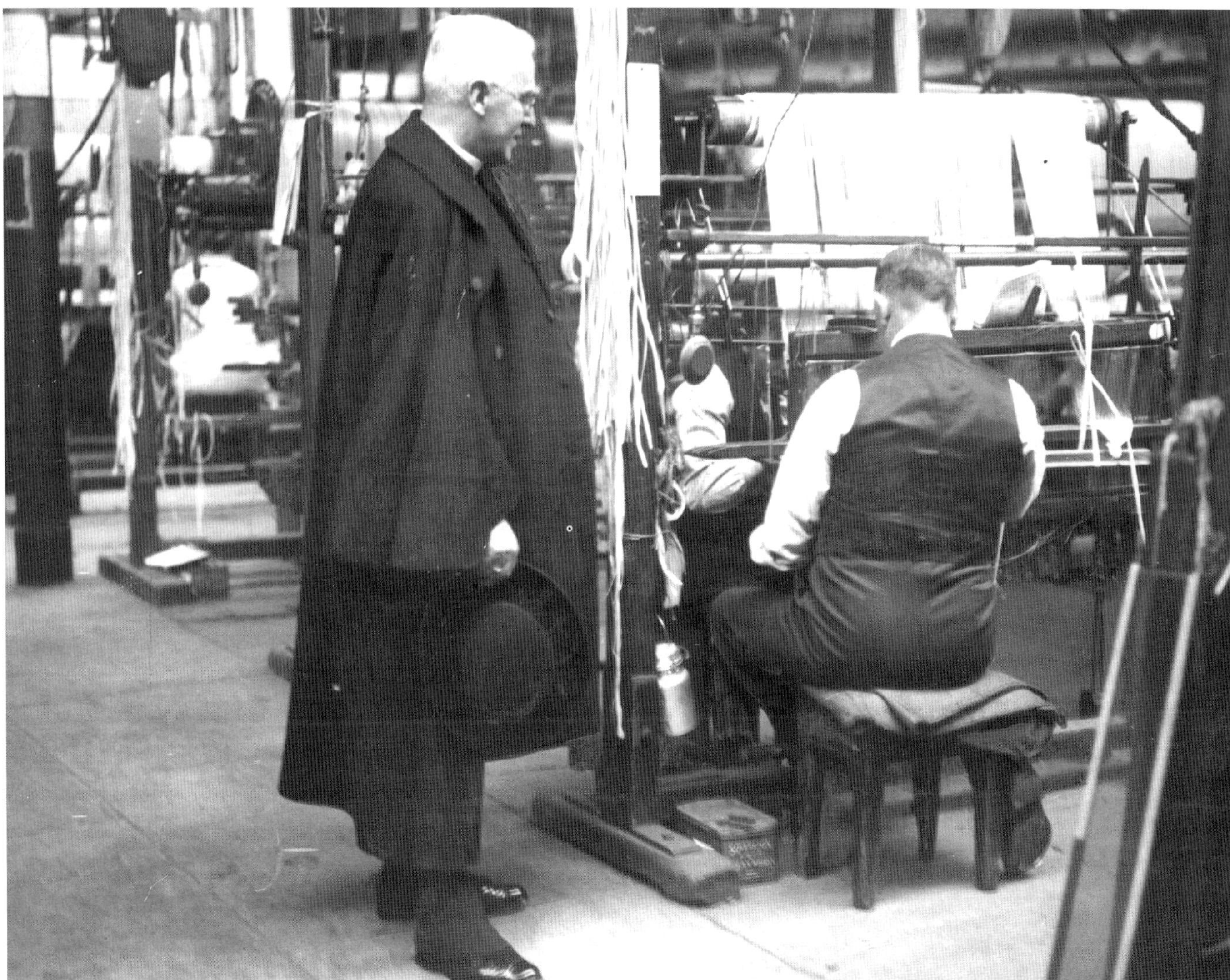

Cardinal Bourne pictured during a visit to discuss working conditions with mill workers in Preston in March 1931.

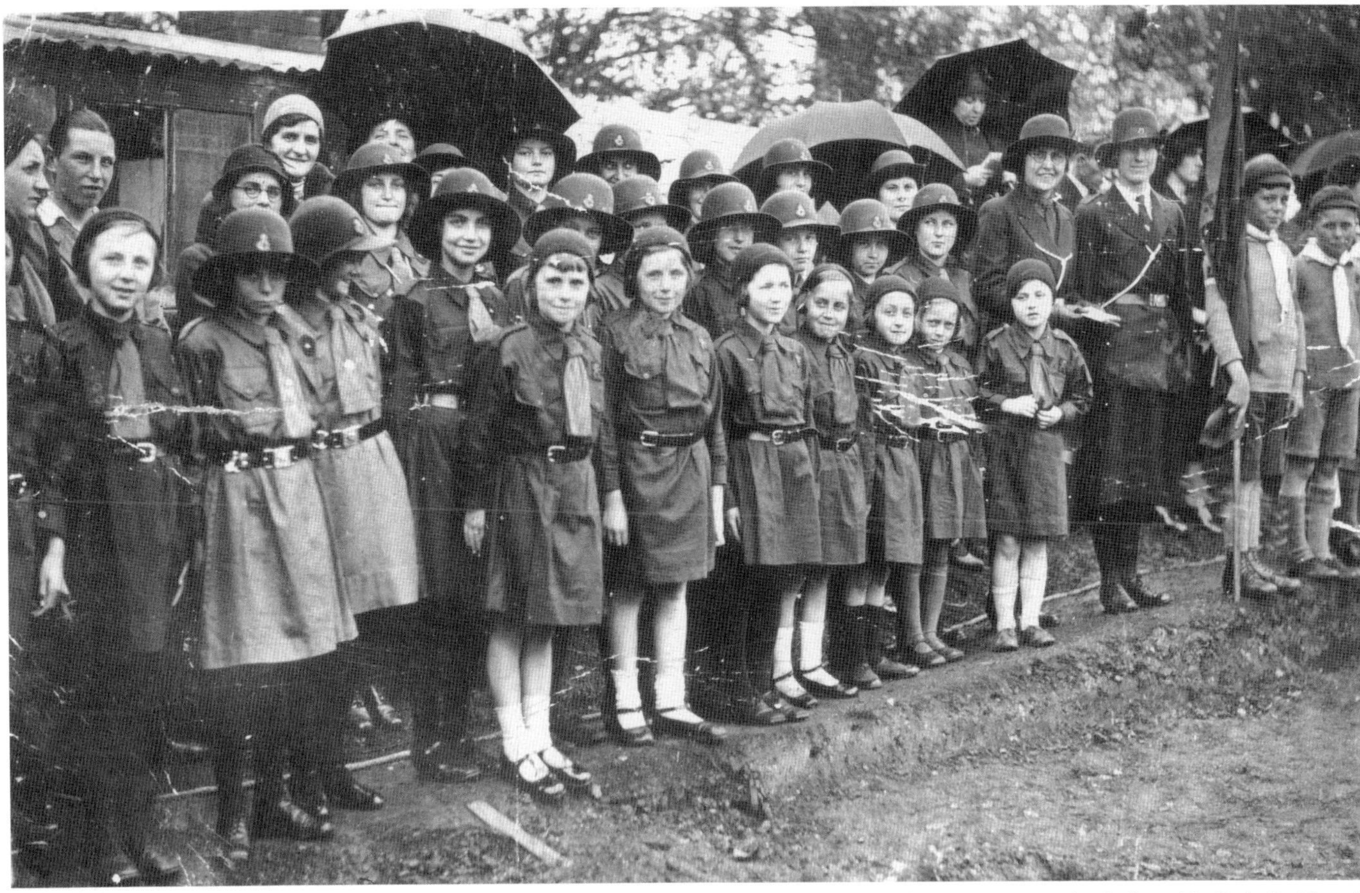

Leaders and members of St. Augustine's Brownie and Guide Pack pictured at the laying of the foundation stone for St. Joseph's Catholic Church, Weymouth, Dorset in 1932.

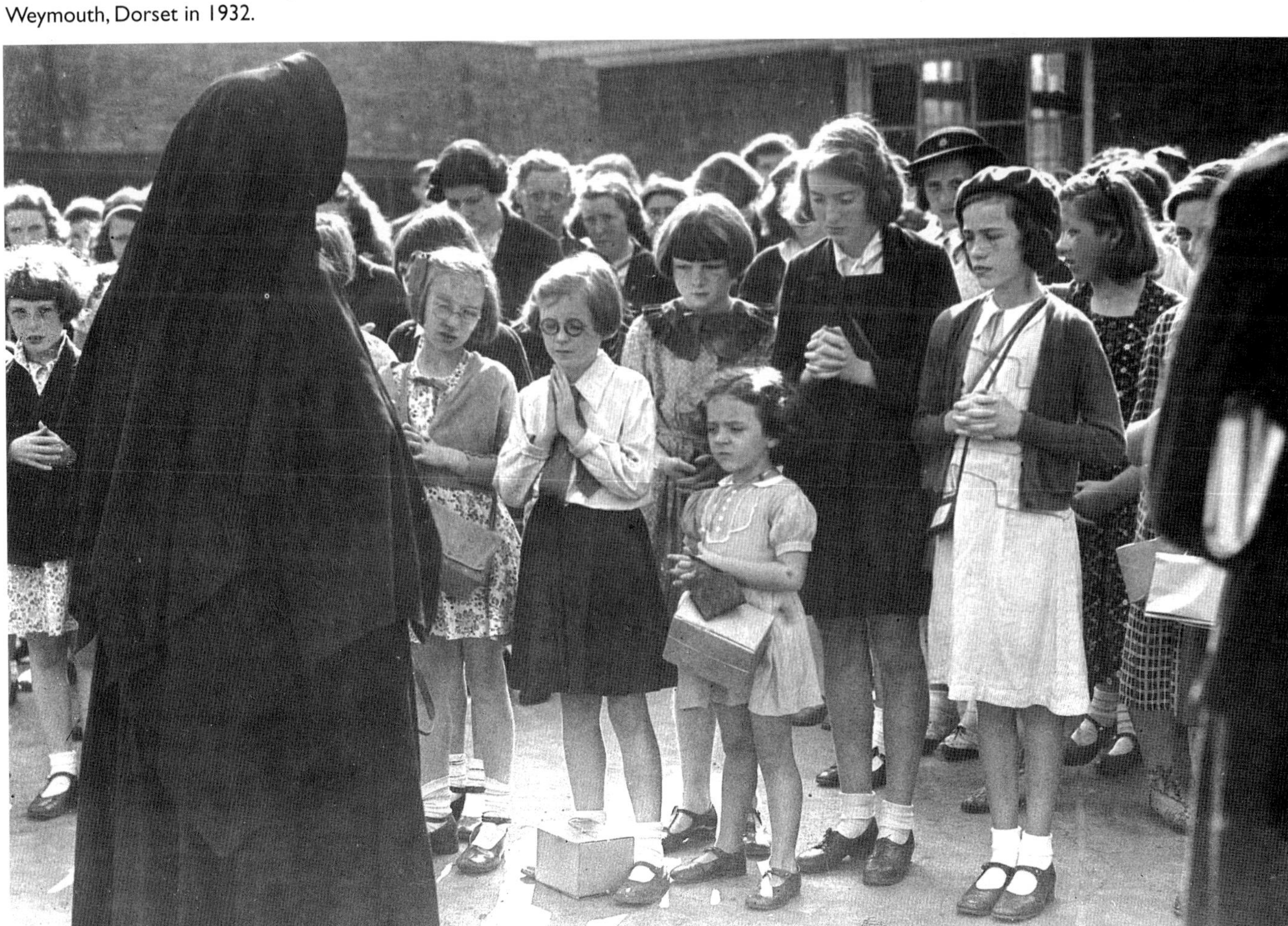

Evacuated children from a north London convent school in September 1939 are pictured at prayers with their teacher, following morning roll-call at their new school "somewhere in the Midlands".

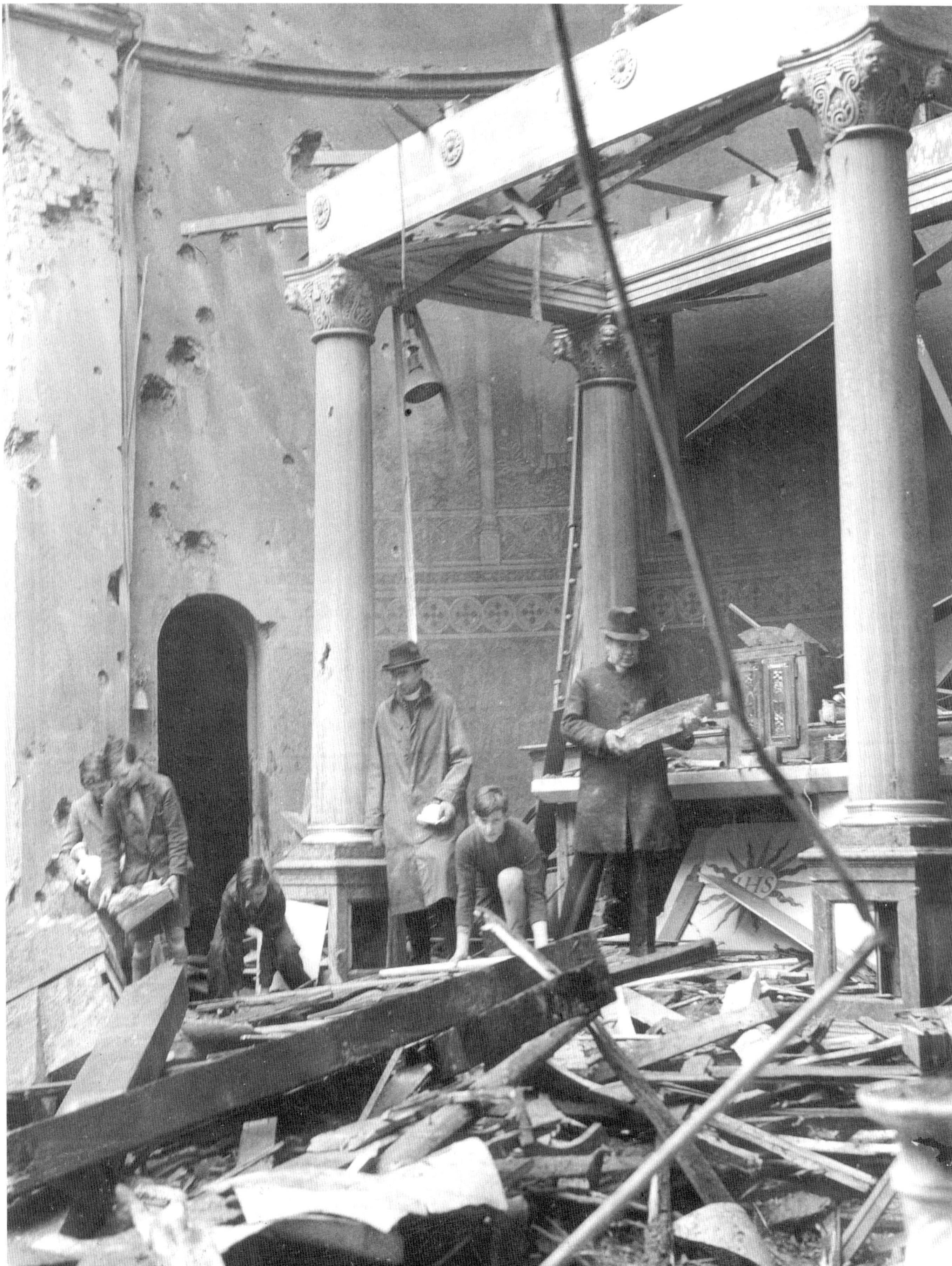

After heavy German bombing of London in April 1941, many churches in the city were left severely damaged. Among them was St. Dominic's, Homerton, where a bomber scored a direct hit on the church, and another fell bomb on the presbytery, where thankfully priests escaped with only minor injuries. In the morning after the attack, Fr. Alphonse Arendzen (right), and his curate Fr. Maurice Kelleher, and a group of young parishioners sift through the debris. (Two copies of this photograph exist in *The Universe* archives; both carry the same information, but the earlier copy names the church as St. Monica's, Homerton. We could find no record of a church of this name in Homerton.)

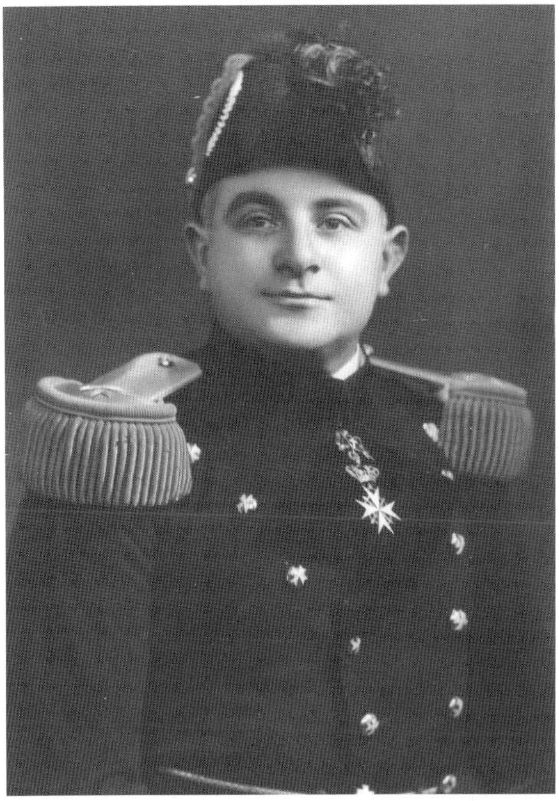

Eoin O Mahony (1904 – 70) was one of modern Ireland's most colourful characters. Eoin was one the O Mahonys of Dun Locha, Douglas, County Cork, and was barrister, Knight of Malta, genealogist, raconteur and a world traveller. It was he who originated the annual O Mahony clan rally in 1955. He was once described as "a maker of epics, an interpreter of history, an incurable romantic, the avowed champion of lost causes, a sterling protagonist of the social values of rural Ireland with a mission of preservation of 'resistance to materialism'." He is pictured here as young man in the uniform of an officer of the Sovereign Order of the Knights of Malta.

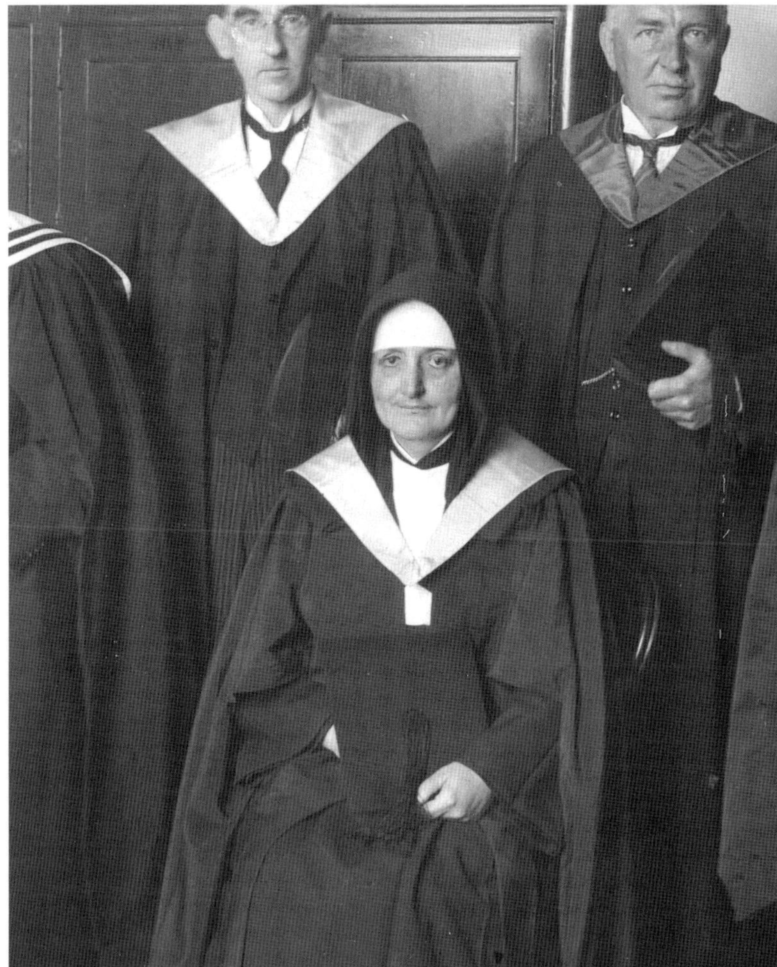

In July 1931 Liverpool University conferred an honorary degree of Master of Arts (*Honoris Causa*) on Wilhelmina Aspel (Sister Imelda) in recognition of her having completed 25 years service as headmistress of Notre Dame Collegiate School, Everton valley, Liverpool, which at the time was the largest secondary school in Merseyside.

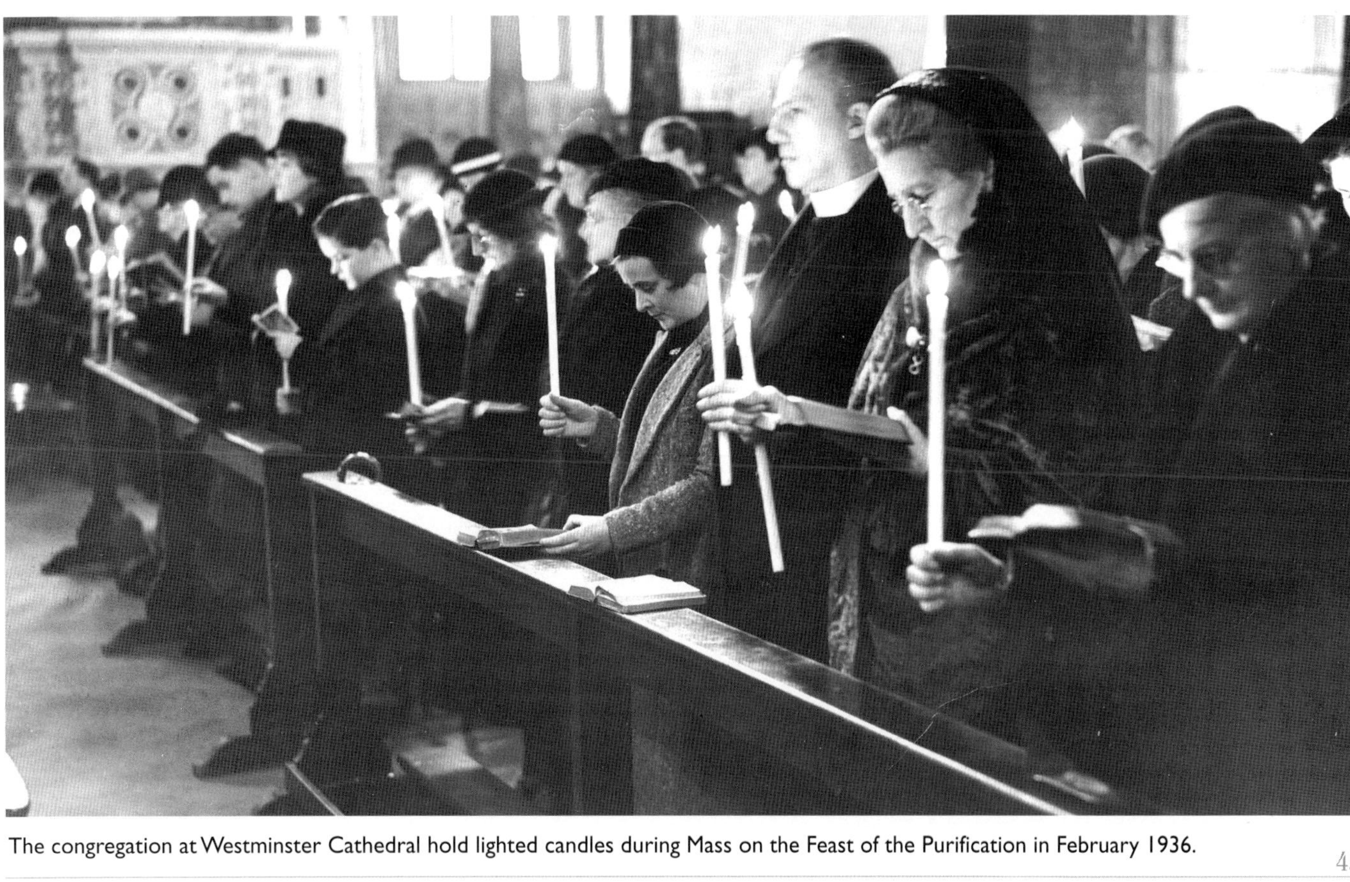

The congregation at Westminster Cathedral hold lighted candles during Mass on the Feast of the Purification in February 1936.

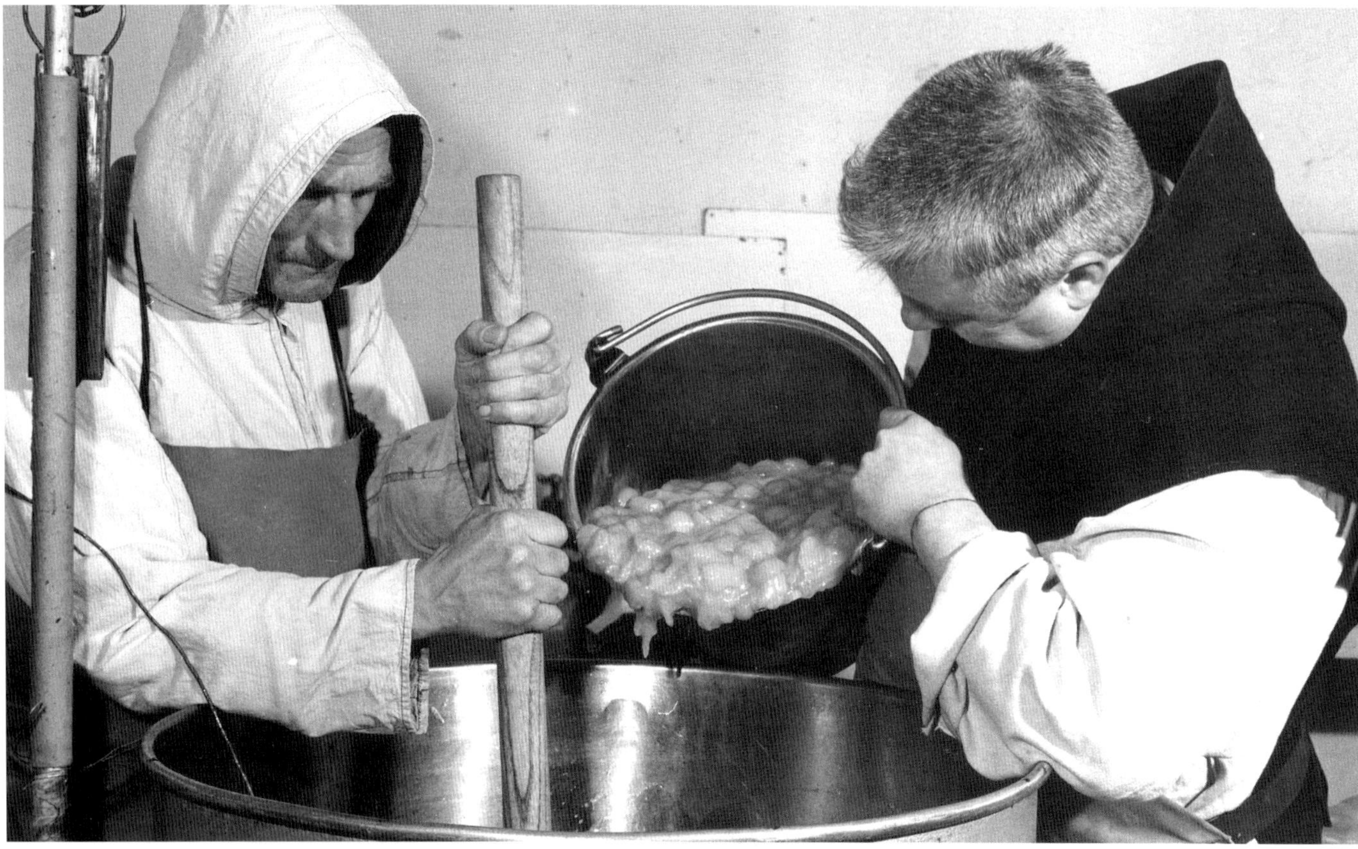

Cistercian monks pour apricot pulp into a steel container for boiling into jam at Mellifont Abbey, Co. Louth in the late 1960s.

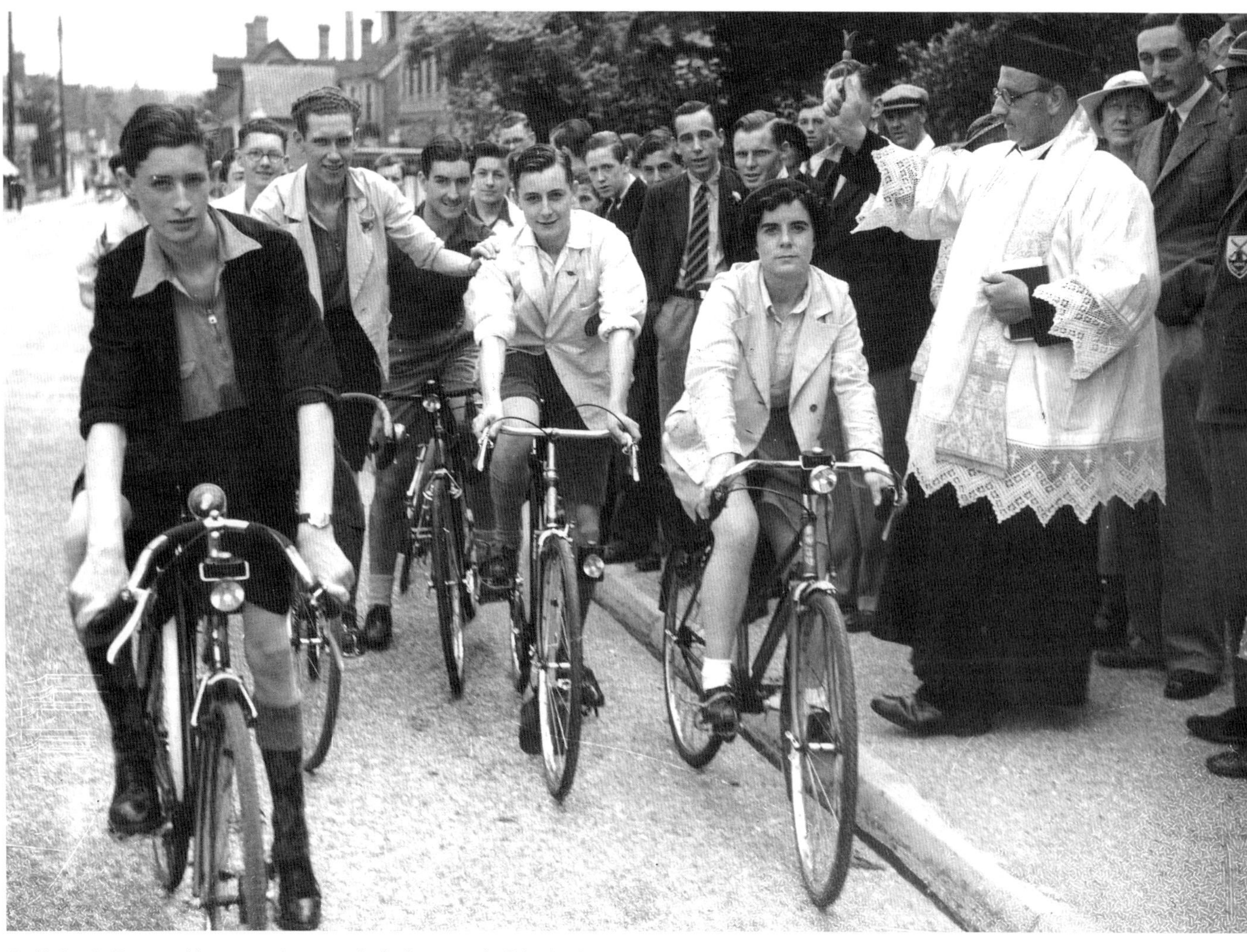

Fr. Philip de Ternant blesses cycles outside St. Laurence's, Edenbridge, Kent, in July 1938, on the Feast of St. Christopher. The day was celebrated with a service for motorists and the blessing of vehicles.

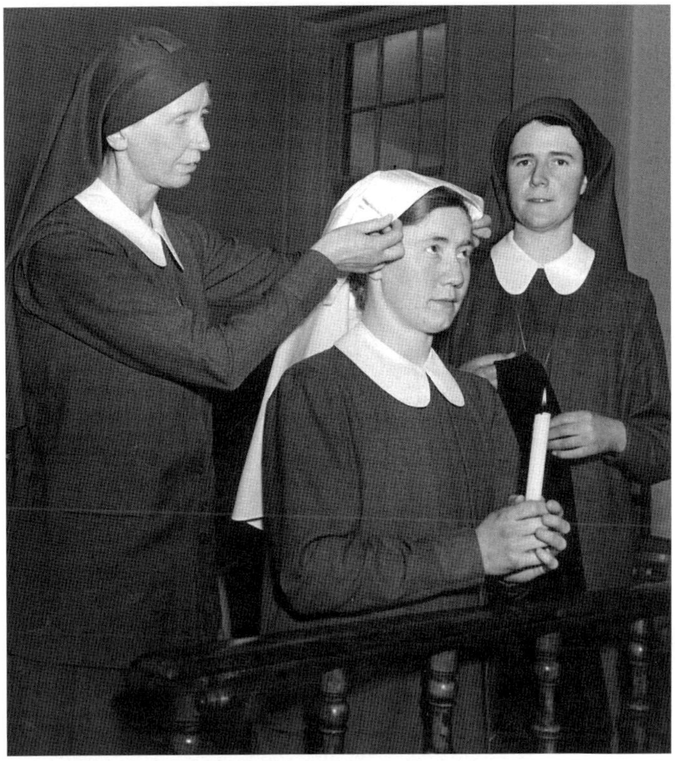

A young woman makes her final profession and receives the habit of the Medical Missionaries of Mary in Drogheda in June 1943 from Mother Mary Martin (left) the foundress of the congregation.

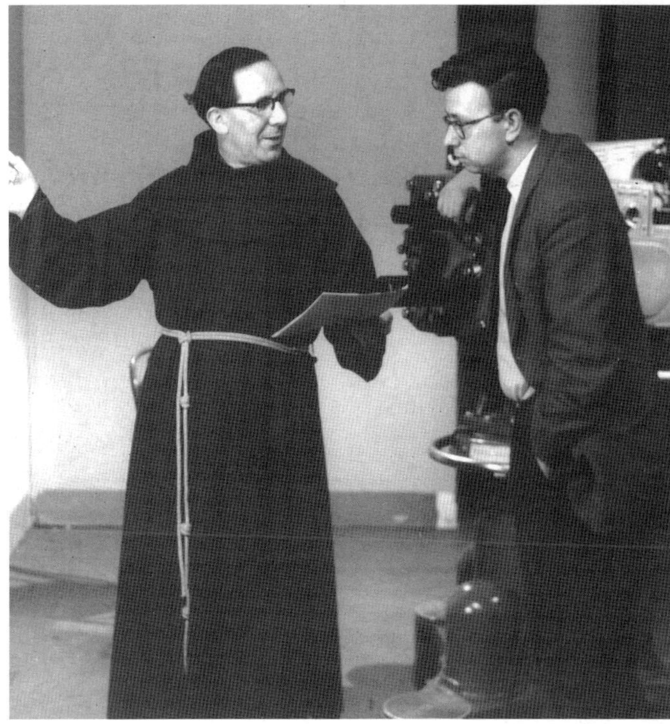

Father (later Bishop) Agnellus Andrew O.F.M. was one of Britain's best-known religious broadcasters. He's pictured here talking with a cameraman in January 1974 at the Catholic Radio and TV Centre, Hatch End, London, of which he was Director.

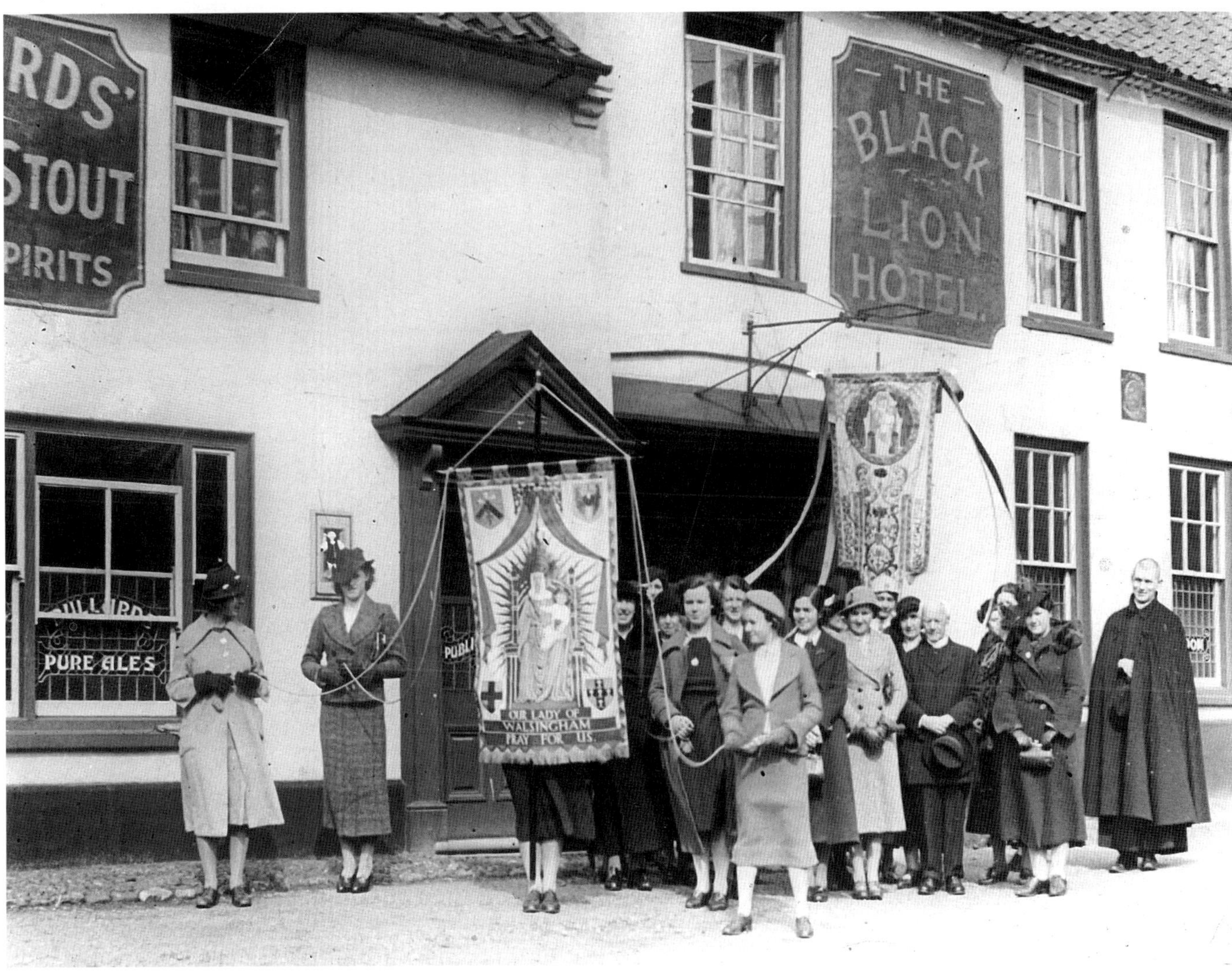

Convent schoolgirls took over the Black Lion, Walsingham, in April 1937, apparently filling it with Catholic pilgrims for the first time since the Reformation. The inn was named after Phillippa, Edward III's queen, after they stayed there on pilgrimage.

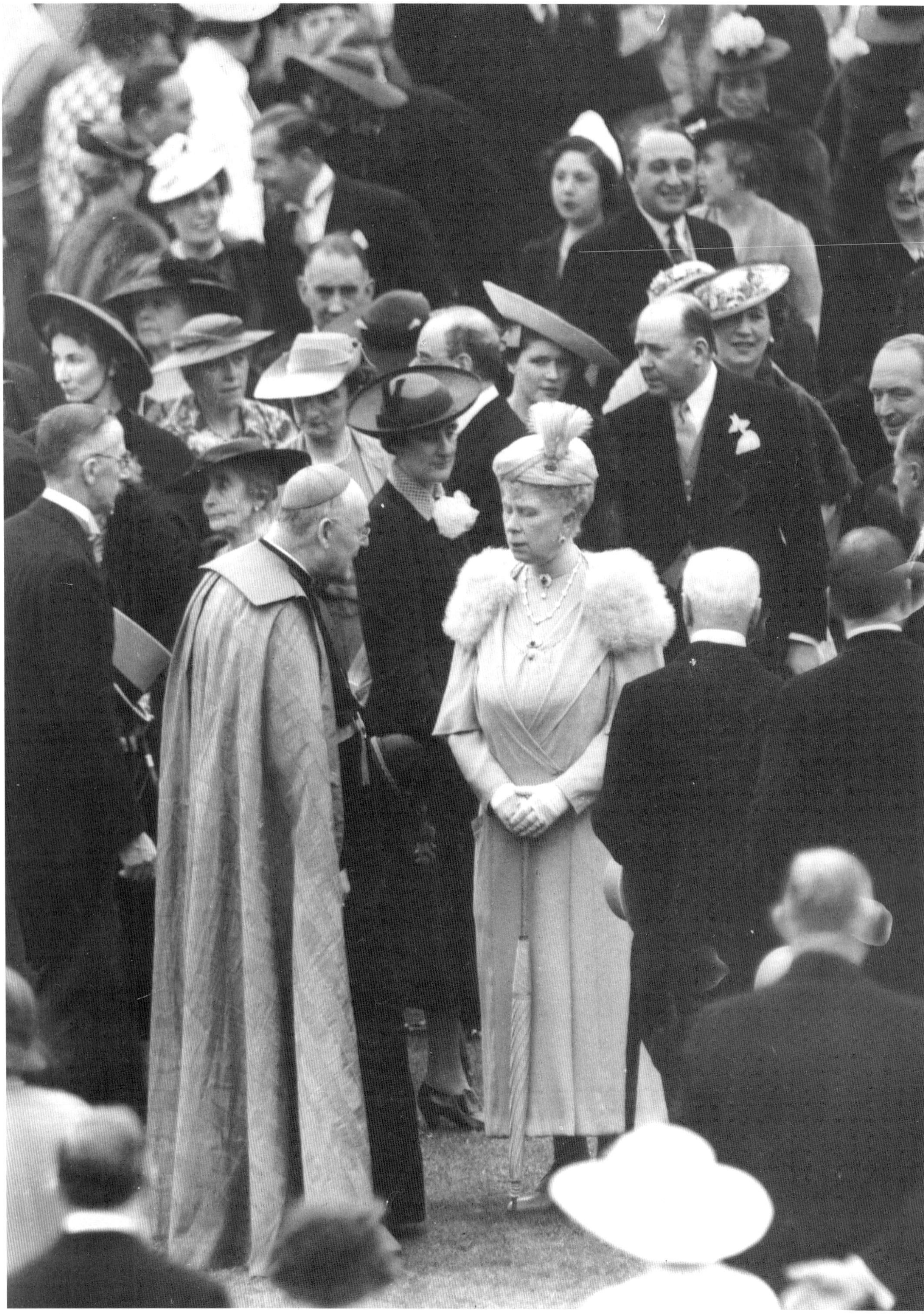

Cardinal Hinsley in conversation with Queen Mary at a garden party in Hampton Court Palace, London in July 1938.

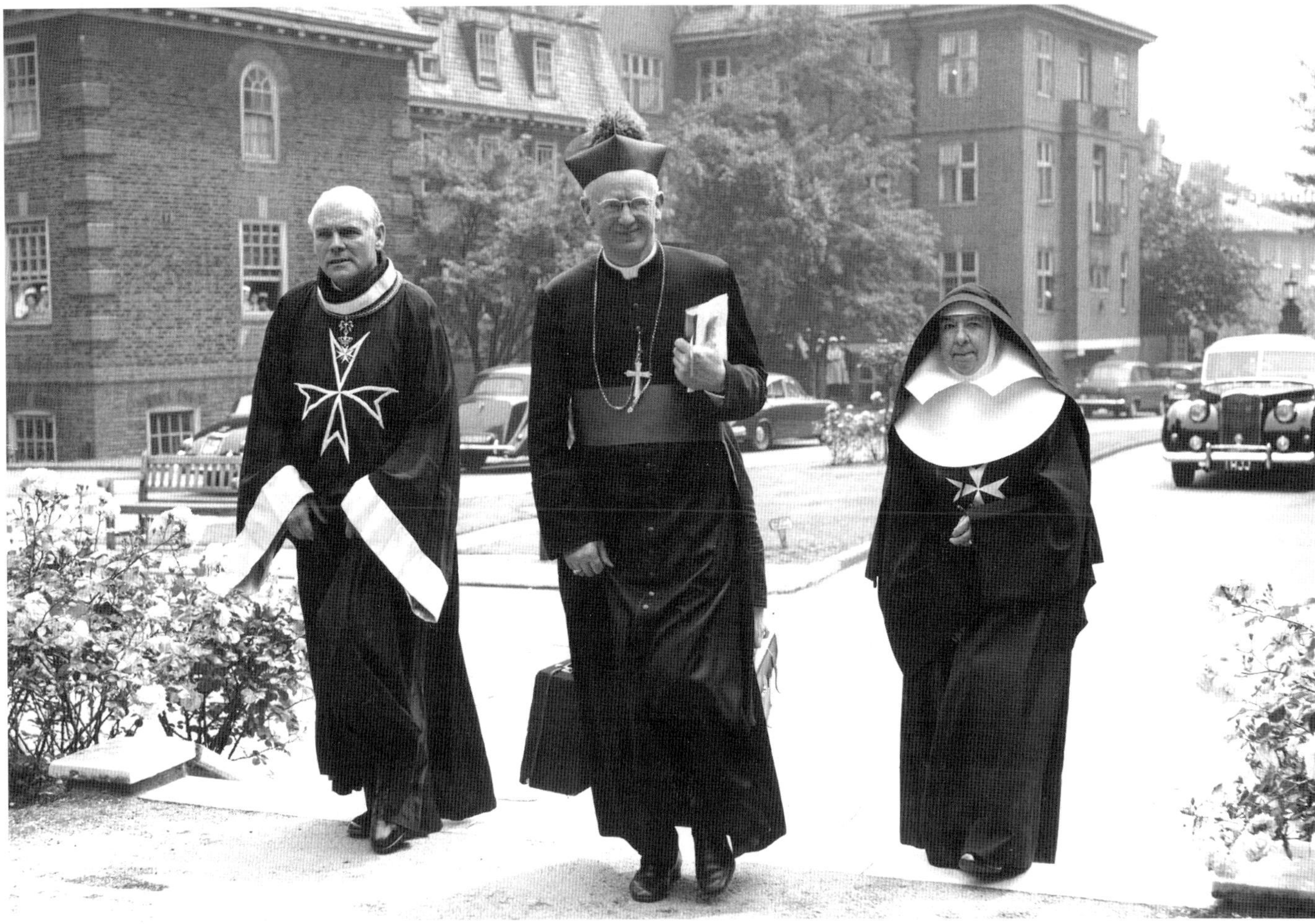

The church of St. John of Jerusalem, Grove End Road, St. John's Wood, London, celebrated the centenary of its opening on 24th June 1964, the Feast of St. John the Baptist. The church was originally built in Great Ormond Street by Sir George Bowyer, for use by the Sisters of Mercy, the patients of the hospital and the Knights of the Order of St. John of Jerusalem. In 1898, when the hospital was moved to its present site at St. John's Wood, the church was transferred stone by stone. Pictured arriving for the centenary service are His Grace Archbishop Heenan of Westminster, the Prioress the Rev. Mother Clare, and Wing Commander R.G. Grant-Ferris MP, Knight of Magistral Grace, the Sovereign and Military Order of Malta.

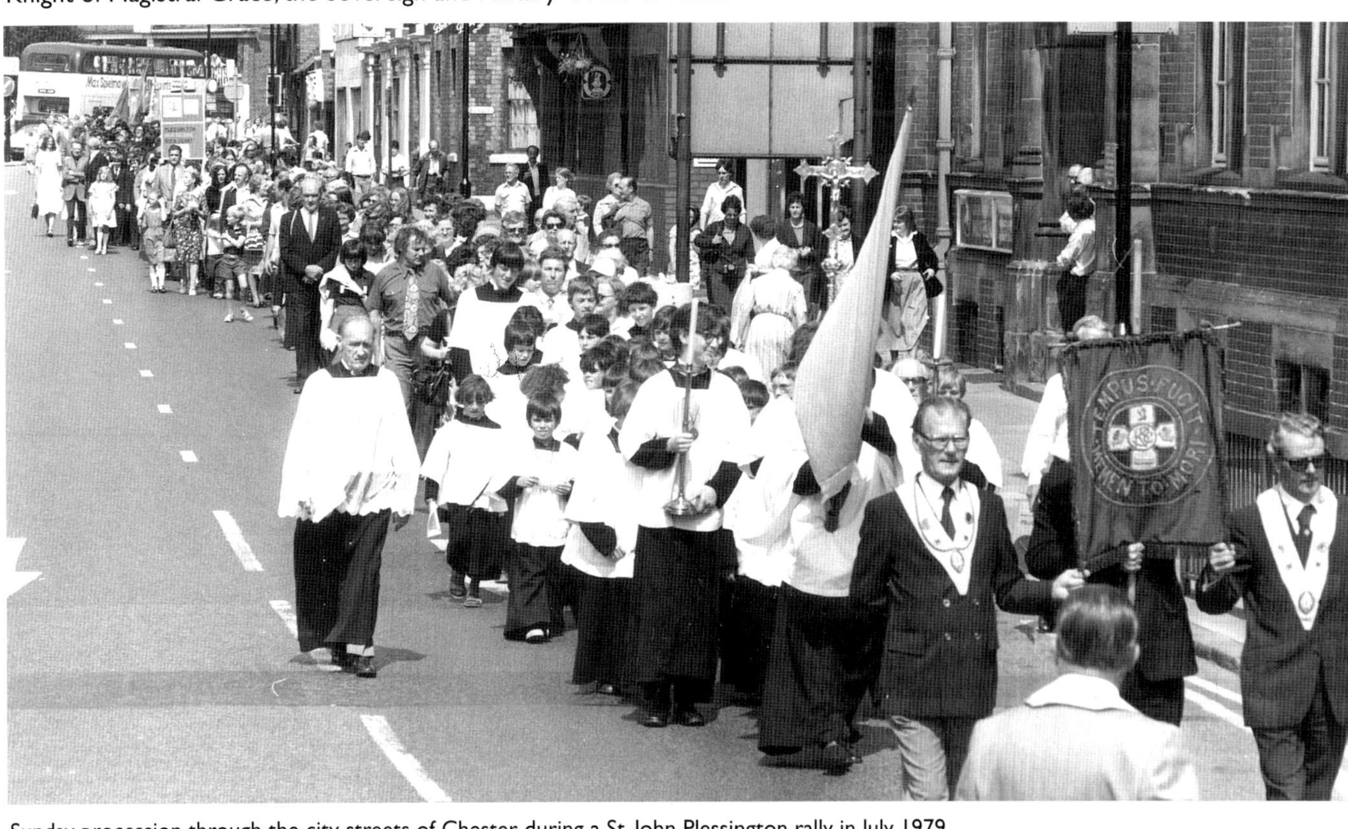

Sunday procession through the city streets of Chester during a St. John Plessington rally in July 1979.

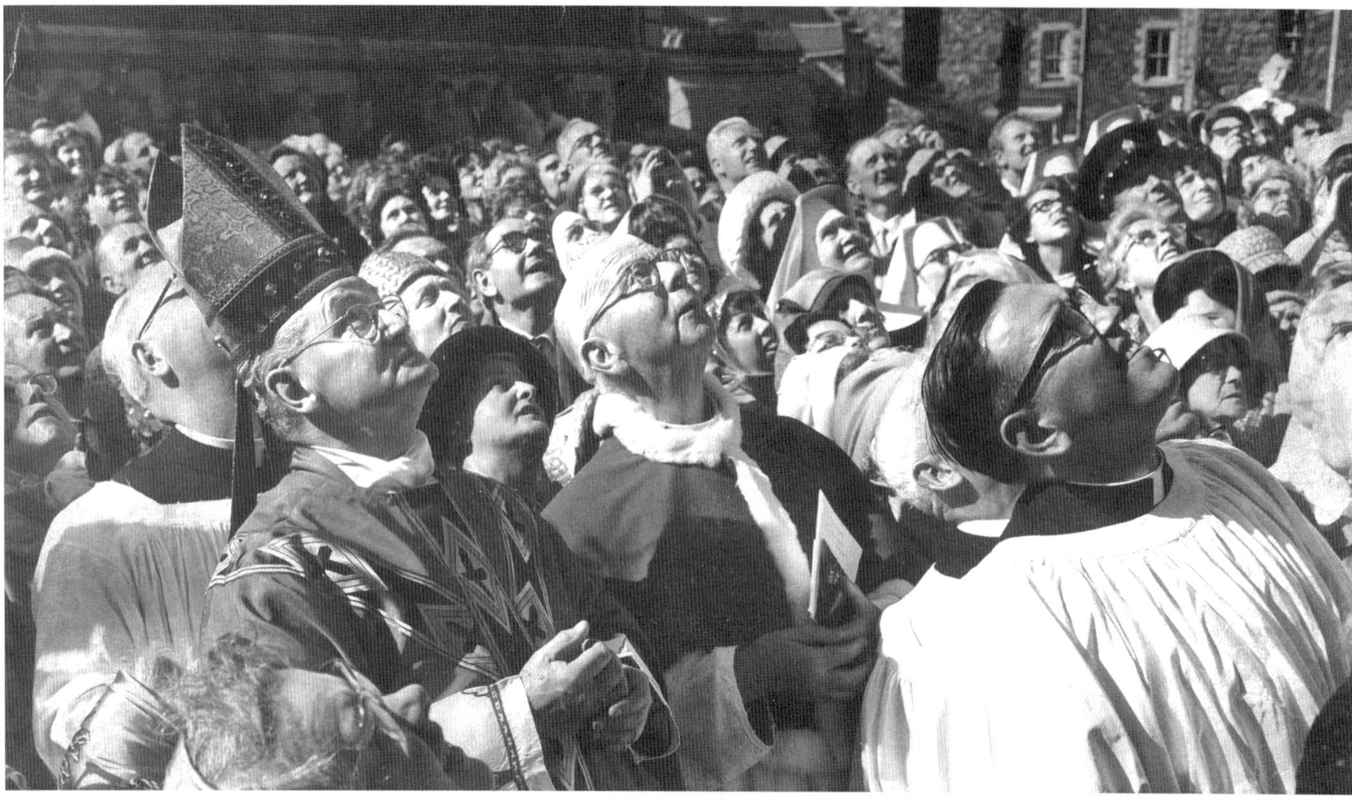

No, it wasn't an air display, but Bishop John Edward Petit of Menevia with priests and people watching the unveiling of a huge crucifix over the main door of the new church at Dolgellau, North Wales in September 1966.

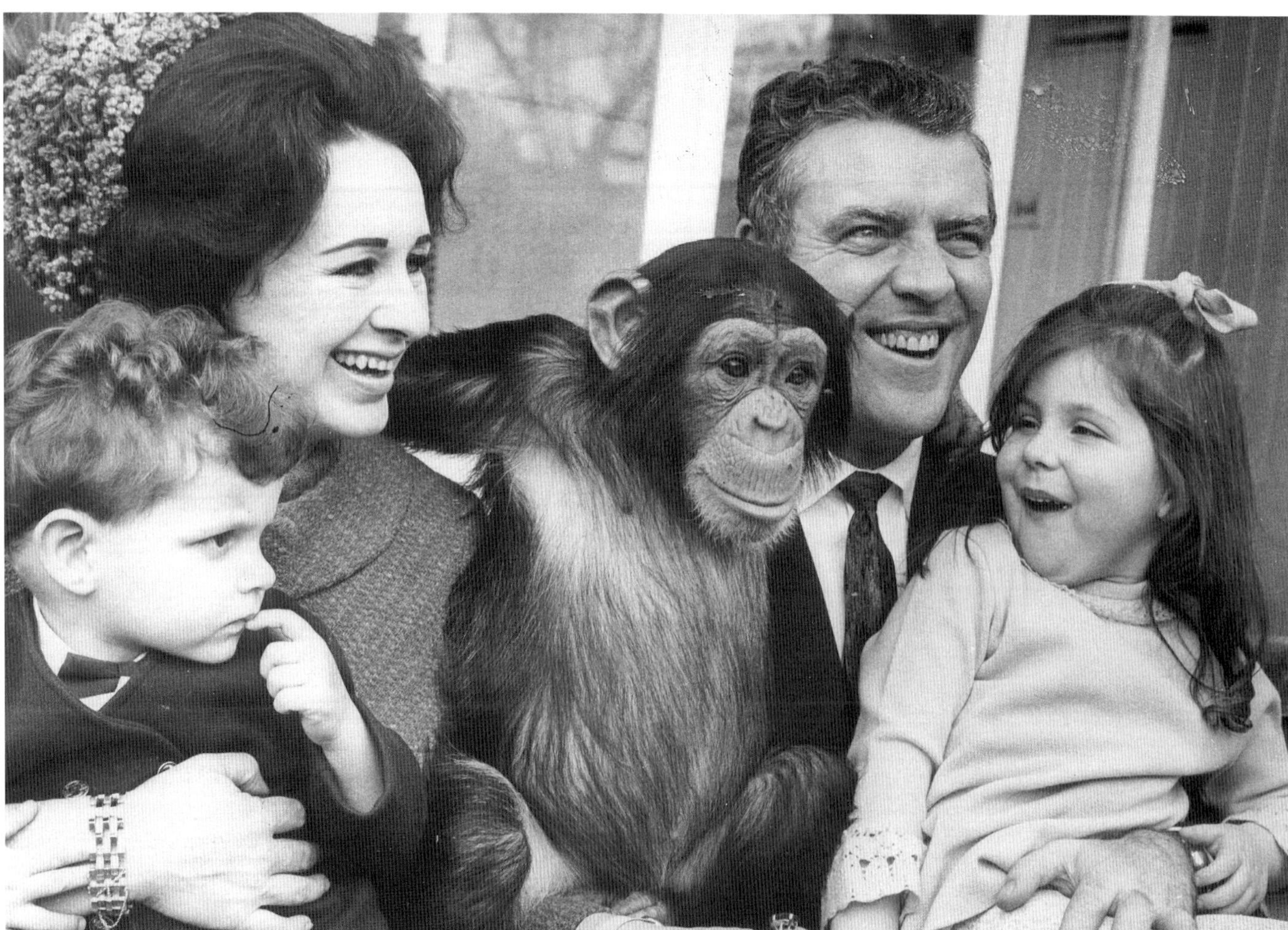

The 14th April 1967 was Grainne Andrews' birthday and husband Eammon decided to take her and the children to London Zoo, where they are seen wowing a chimpanzee called Mary. At the time Eamonn was not only host of TV shows *World of Sport* and *The Eamonn Andrews Show*, but he also found time to pen a weekly sports column for *The Universe*. (*From left*) Eamonn's son Fergal, Grainne, Mary, Eamonn and daughter Emma.

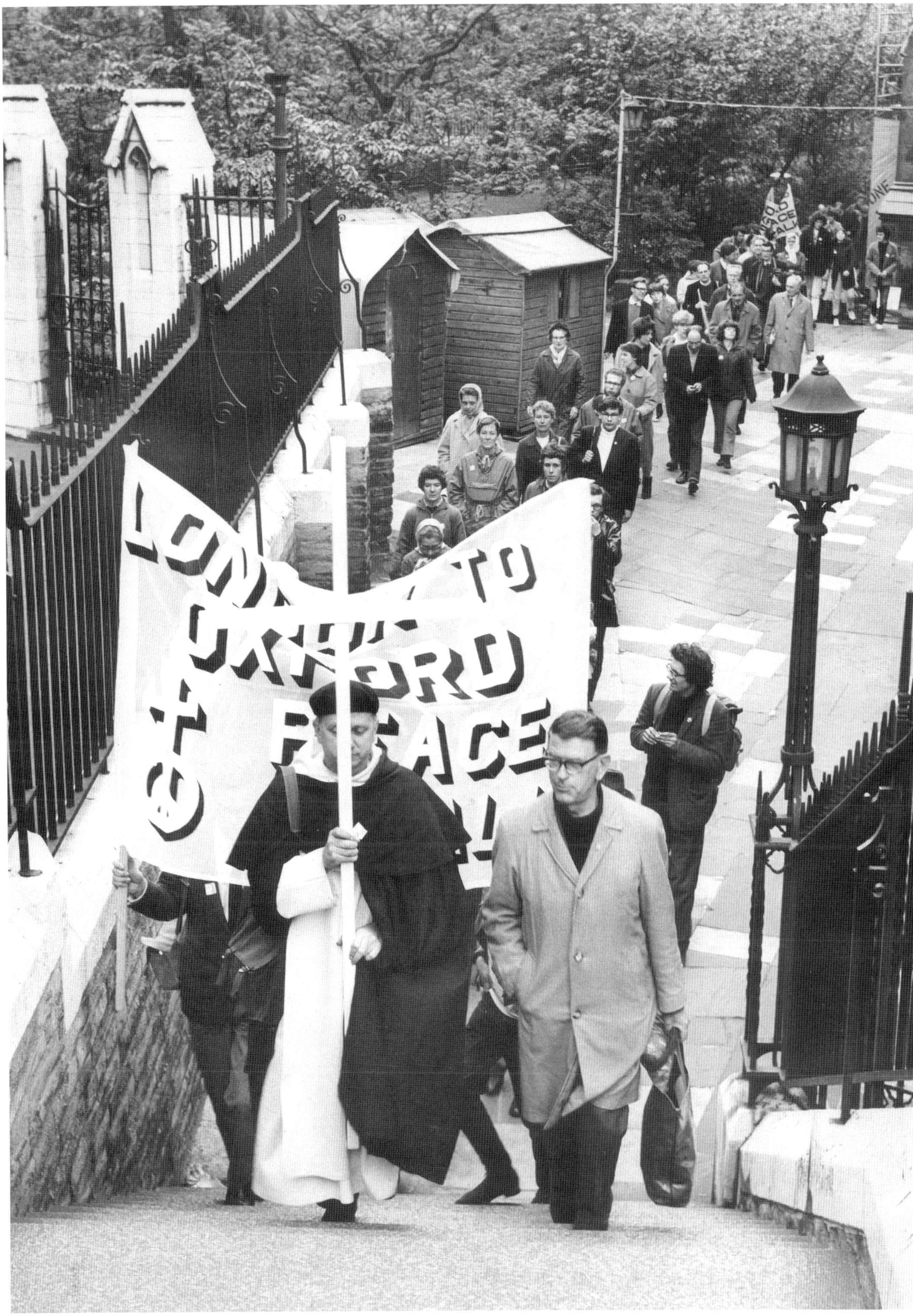

Father Simon Blake, O.P., leads a peace walk from London's Southwark Cathedral to St. Giles, Blackfriars, Oxford in May 1967.

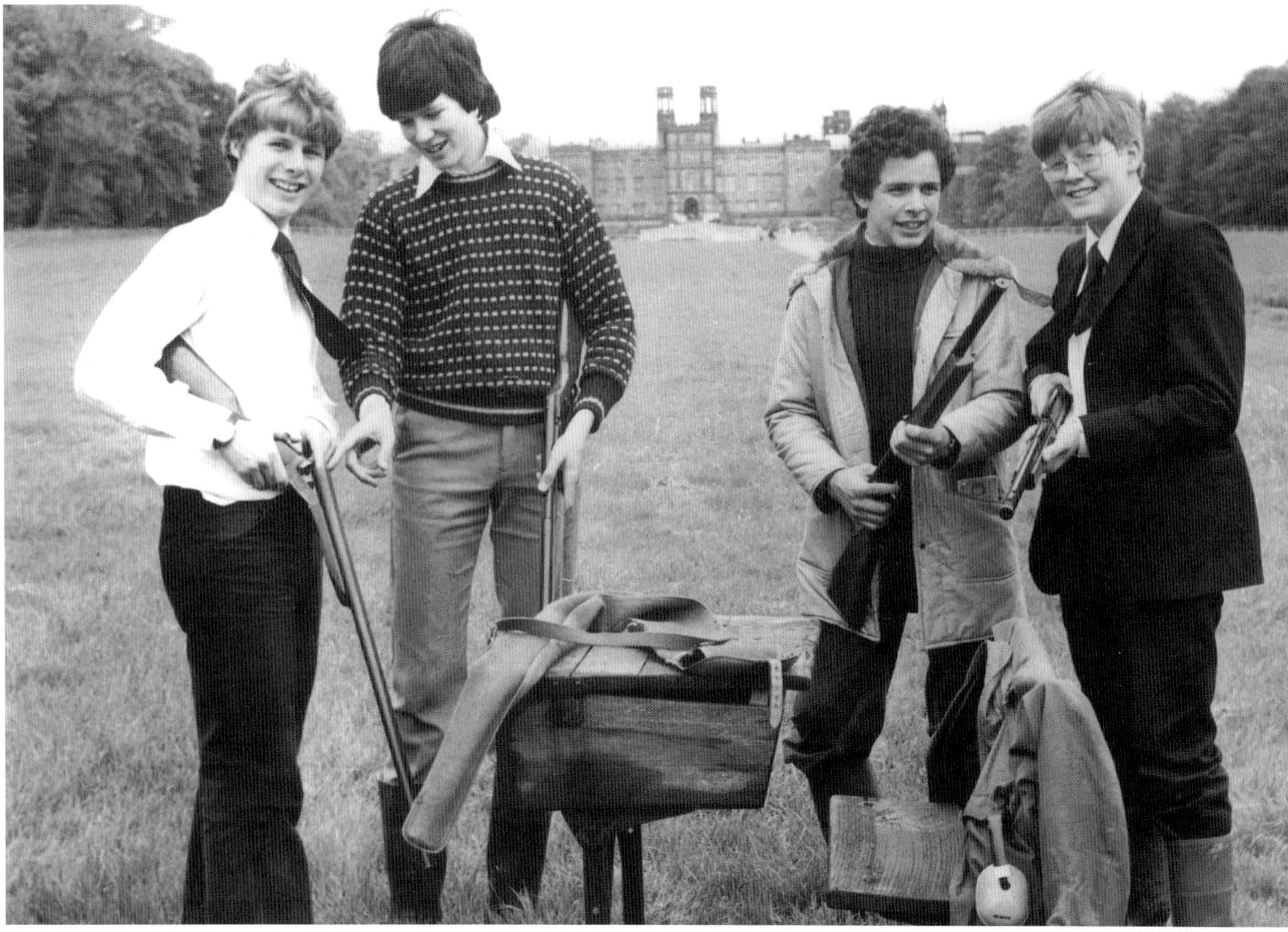

Pupils of Stonyhurst College near Blackburn, Lancs, pictured at the clay pigeon shooting range at the college annual open day in June 1976. (From left) Tony Rowland, Leo Hermacinski, Jacques du Chastel and John Lloyd.

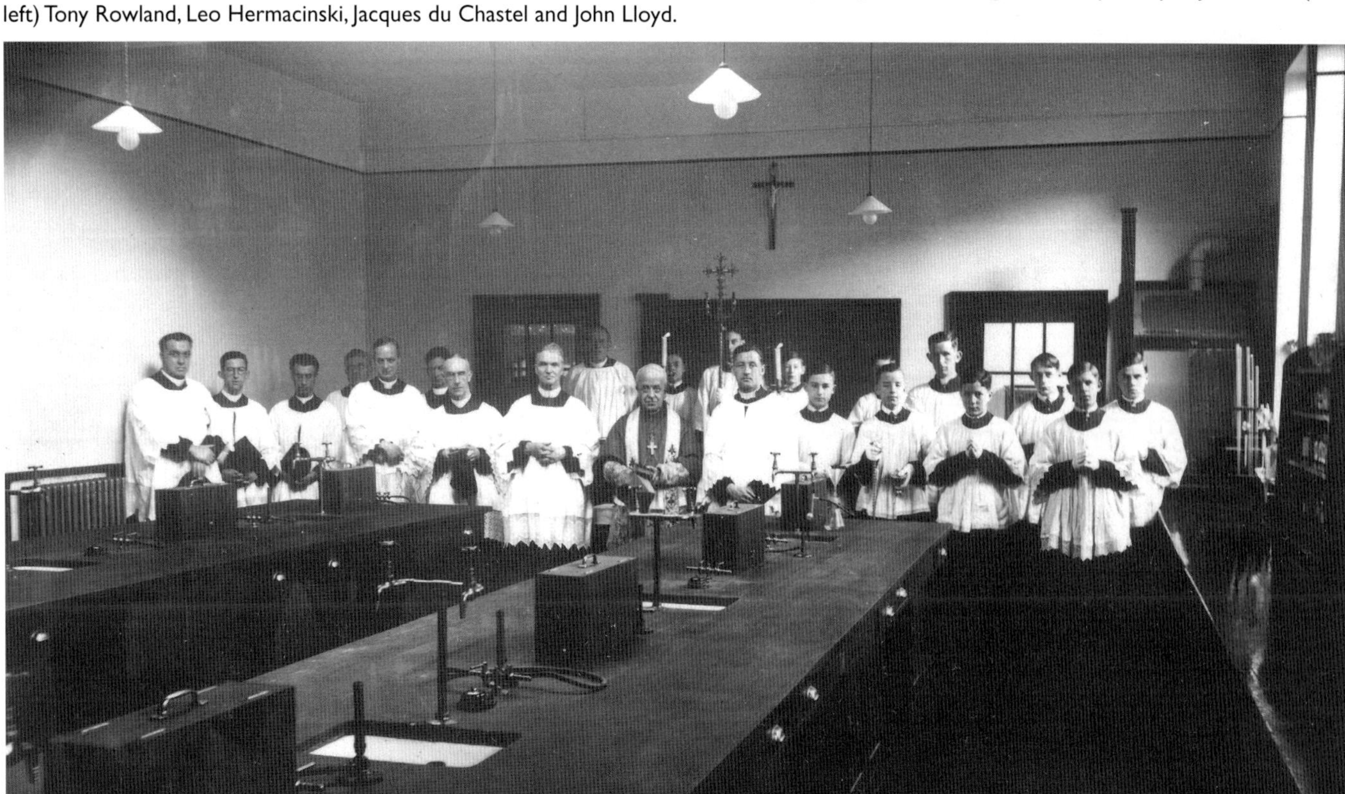

Bishop Dunne of Nottingham opening the new science laboratory at Ratcliffe College, Leicester, in January 1931. Ratcliffe College is an independent Catholic boarding and day school situated on the Fosse Way about six miles north of Leicester. It was founded on the instructions of Fr. Antonio Rosmini-Serbati in 1845 as a seminary. In 1847, the buildings were converted for use as a boarding school for boys. The College became coeducational in the mid 1970s. The College buildings were designed by the Victorian Gothic revivalist Augustus Welby Pugin, and its Square was designed by Joseph Hansom, the designer of the Hansom cab.

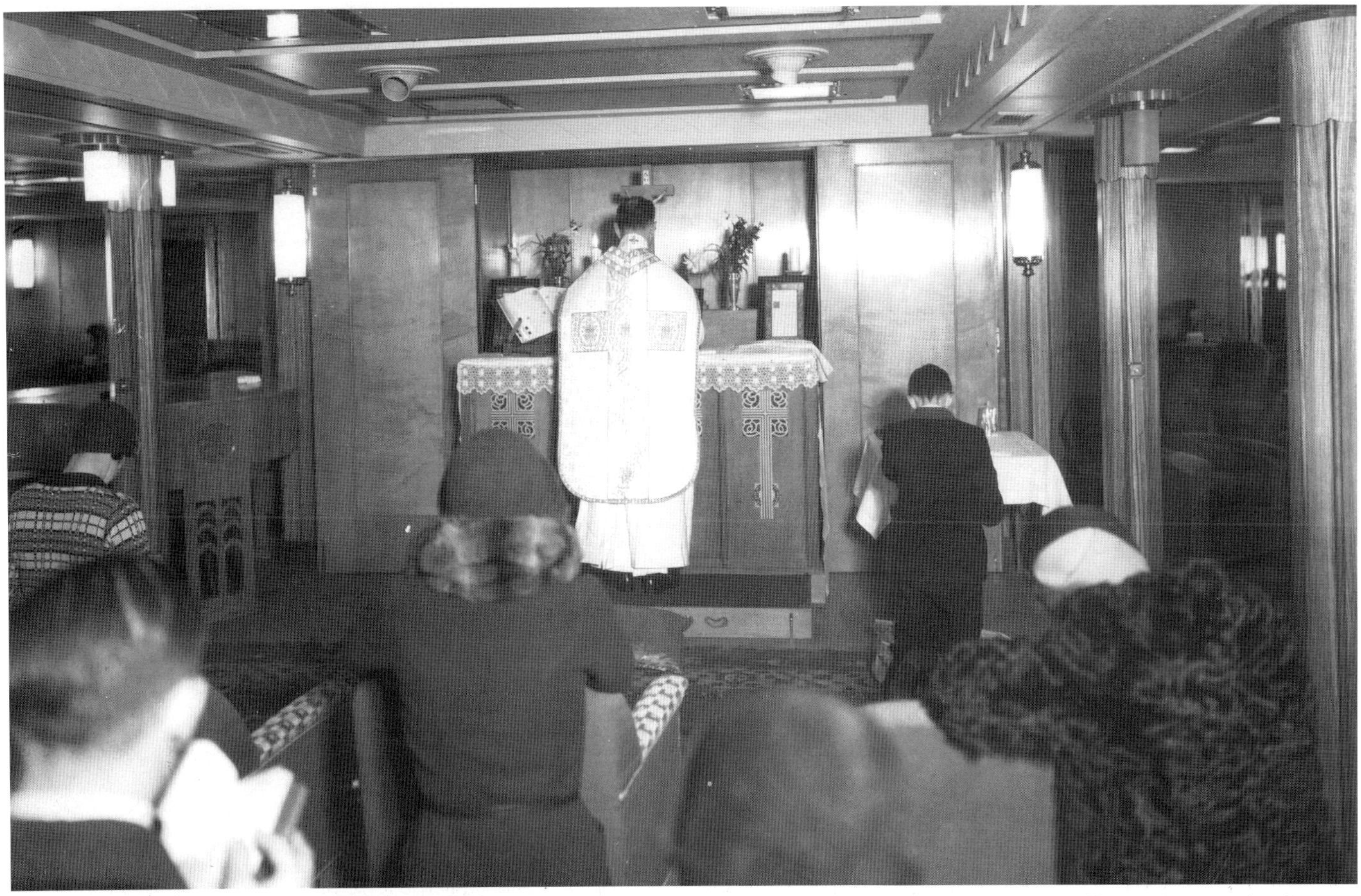

Mass being celebrated in mid-Atlantic on the newly-launched Canadian Pacific liner, *RMS Empress of Britain*, in July 1931. At the time the ship was on its second journey between Southampton and Quebec, during which she set a new record for the Atlantic crossing. Sadly this great ship was lost in October 1940 after being divebombed by the Luftwaffe off the north west coast of Ireland.

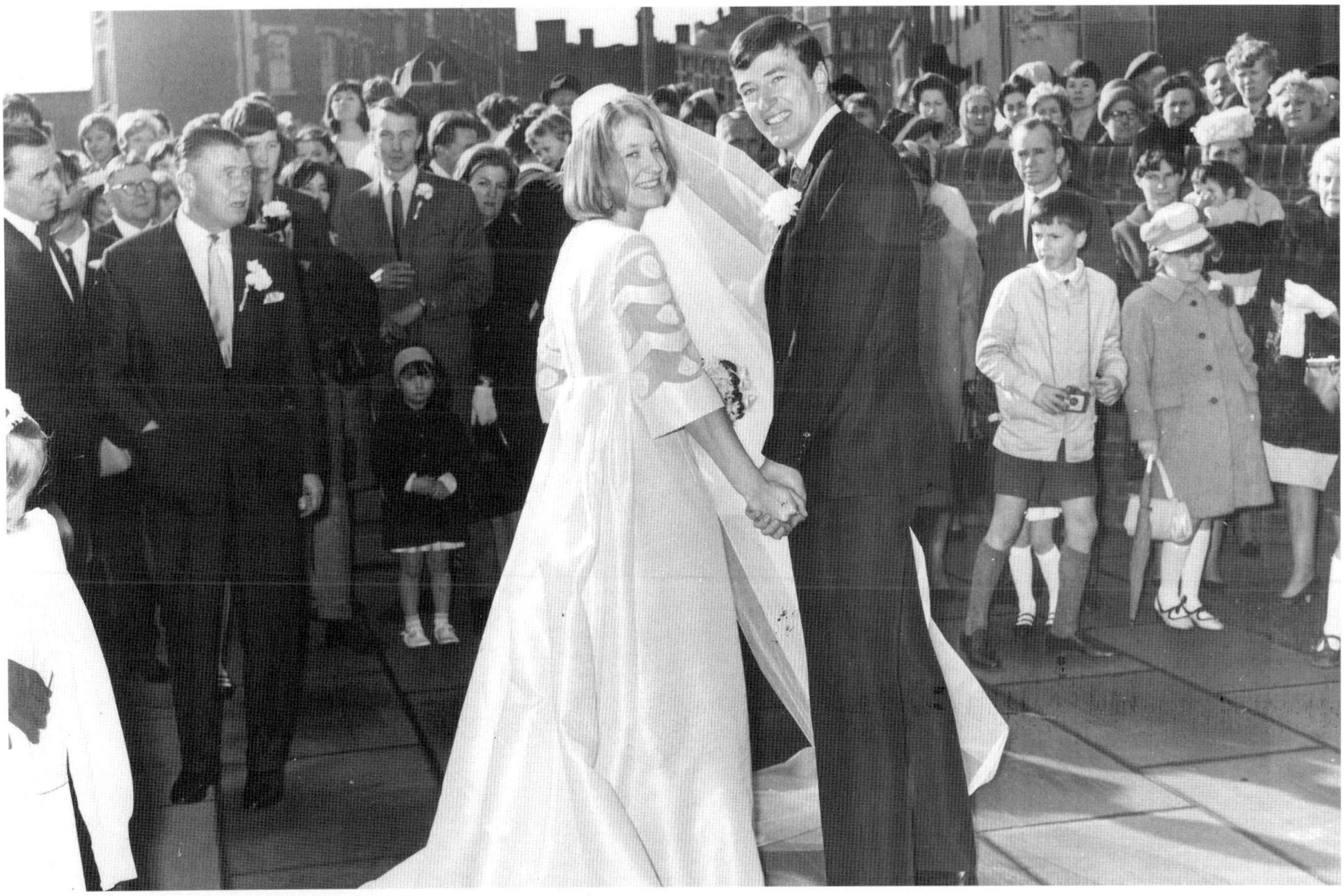

Mr. (later Baron) Bob Mellish, Parliamentary Secretary to the Minister of Housing, looks on as his son, P.C. David Mellish, leaves Holy Trinity Church, Dockhead, London in April 1967, after his marriage to Miss Mary Leahy. Mr. Mellish Snr was married in the same church 28 years earlier. A long-serving Labour MP and ardent Millwall supporter, Baron Mellish died on 10th May 1998.

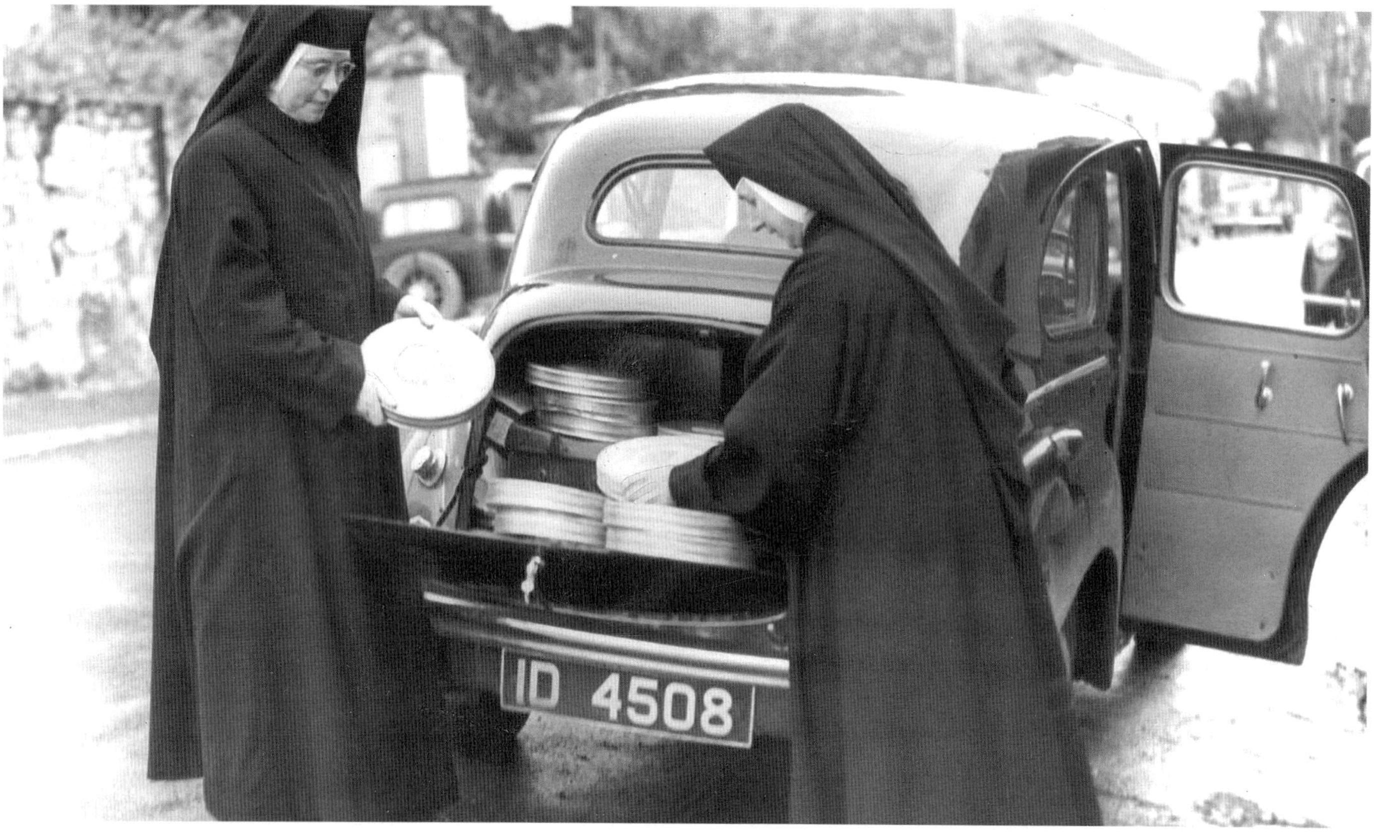

Two sisters from the Holy Rosary Missionary Convent, Killeshandra, Co. Cavan, pack cans containing 12,000ft of film into their car after showing it at Fermoy, Co. Cork in November 1950. They were on a tour of the south of ireland with the film *Out of Darkness*, driving their own car and arranging their own publicity.

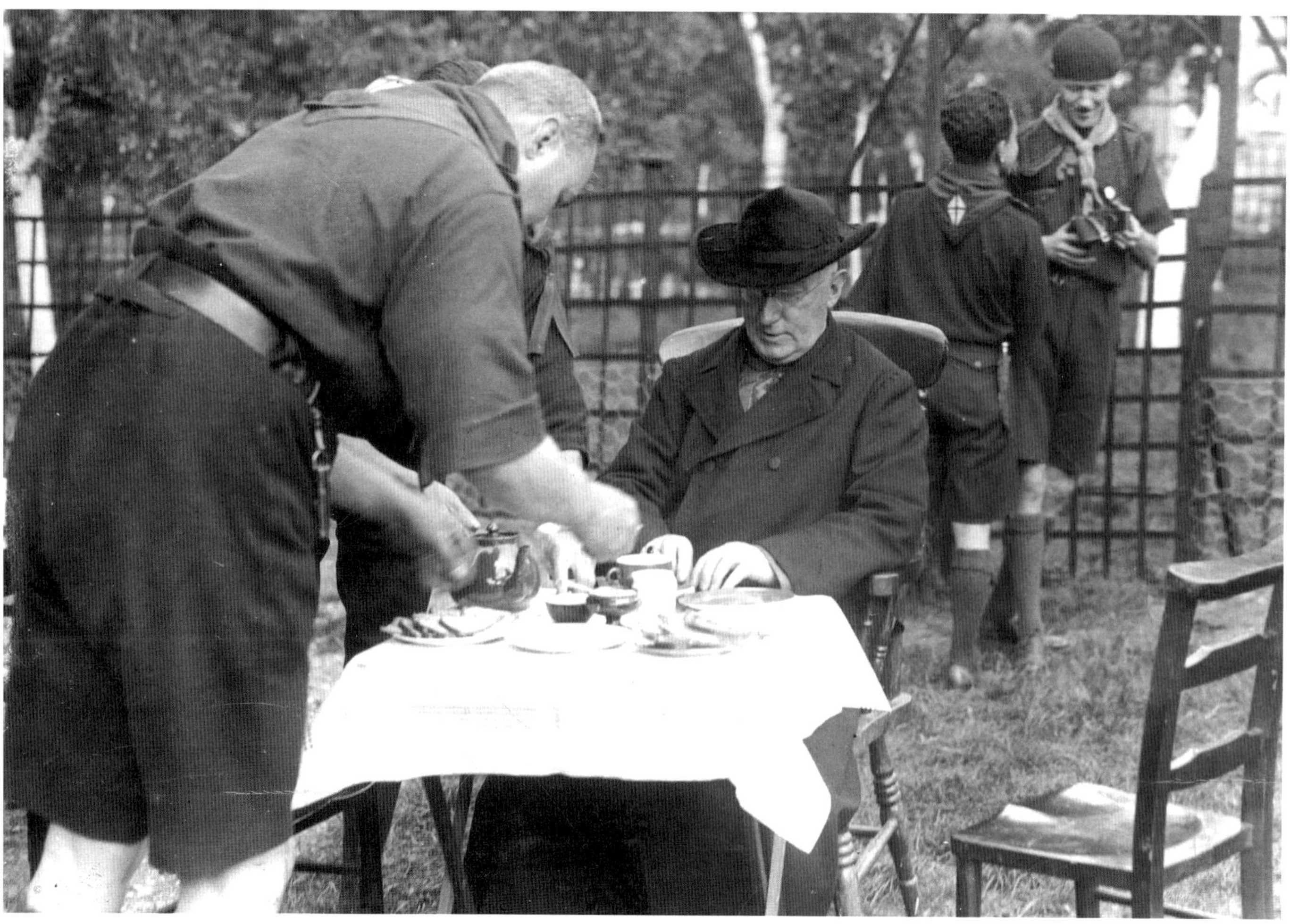

A charmingly informal snapshot of Cardinal Bourne at tea in a Scout camp in September 1926. The cardinal joined the Scouts as they celebrated a reunion for members who had gone on a special pilgrimage to Rome the previous year.

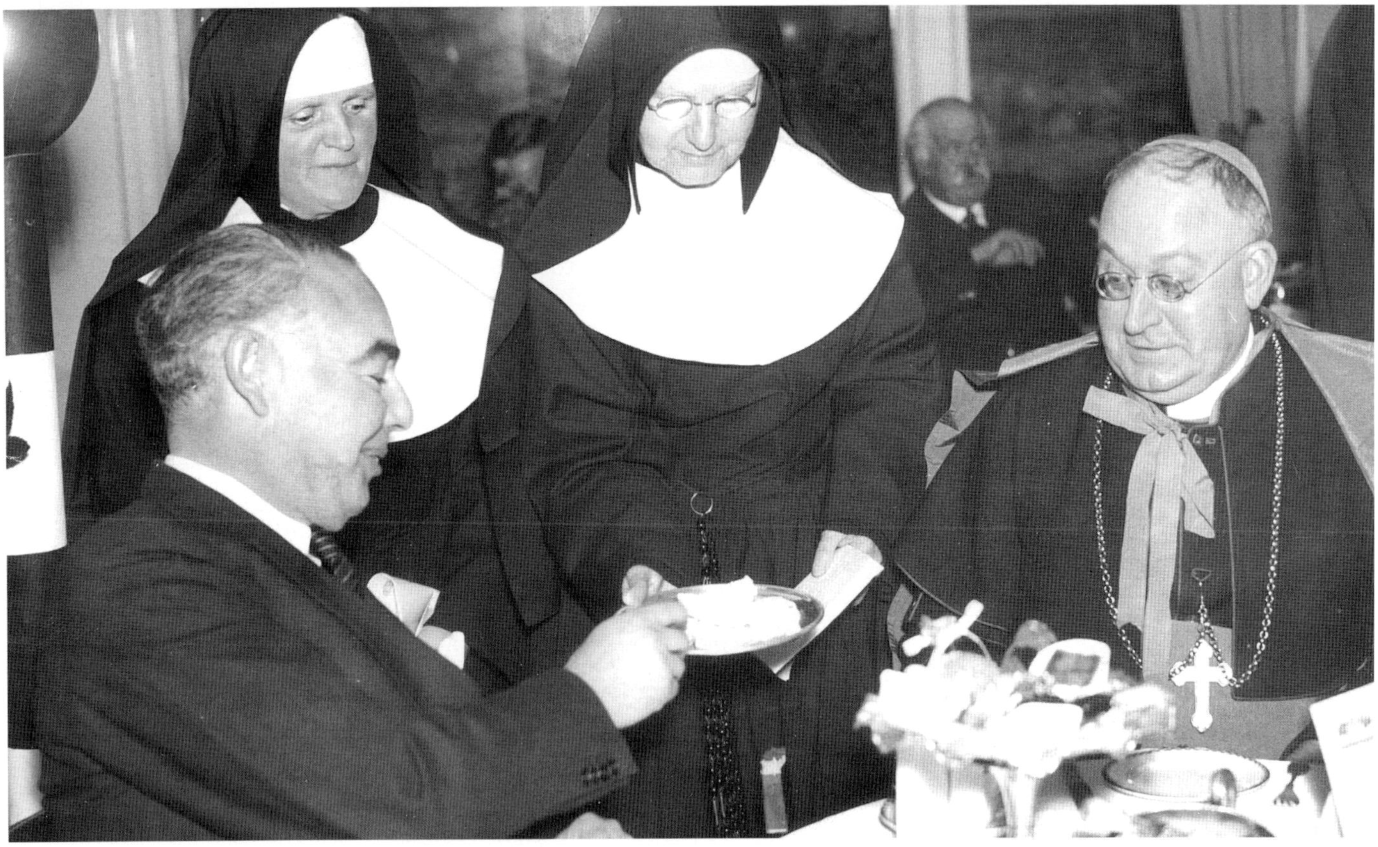

Mr. Hore-Belisha, Minister for War (who lent his name to the orange traffic beacons he introduced in 1934) enjoys tea with Bishop Barrett of Plymouth after opening an extension at Plymouth's Notre Dame High School in December 1938. Note the Belisha beacon to left of the picture!

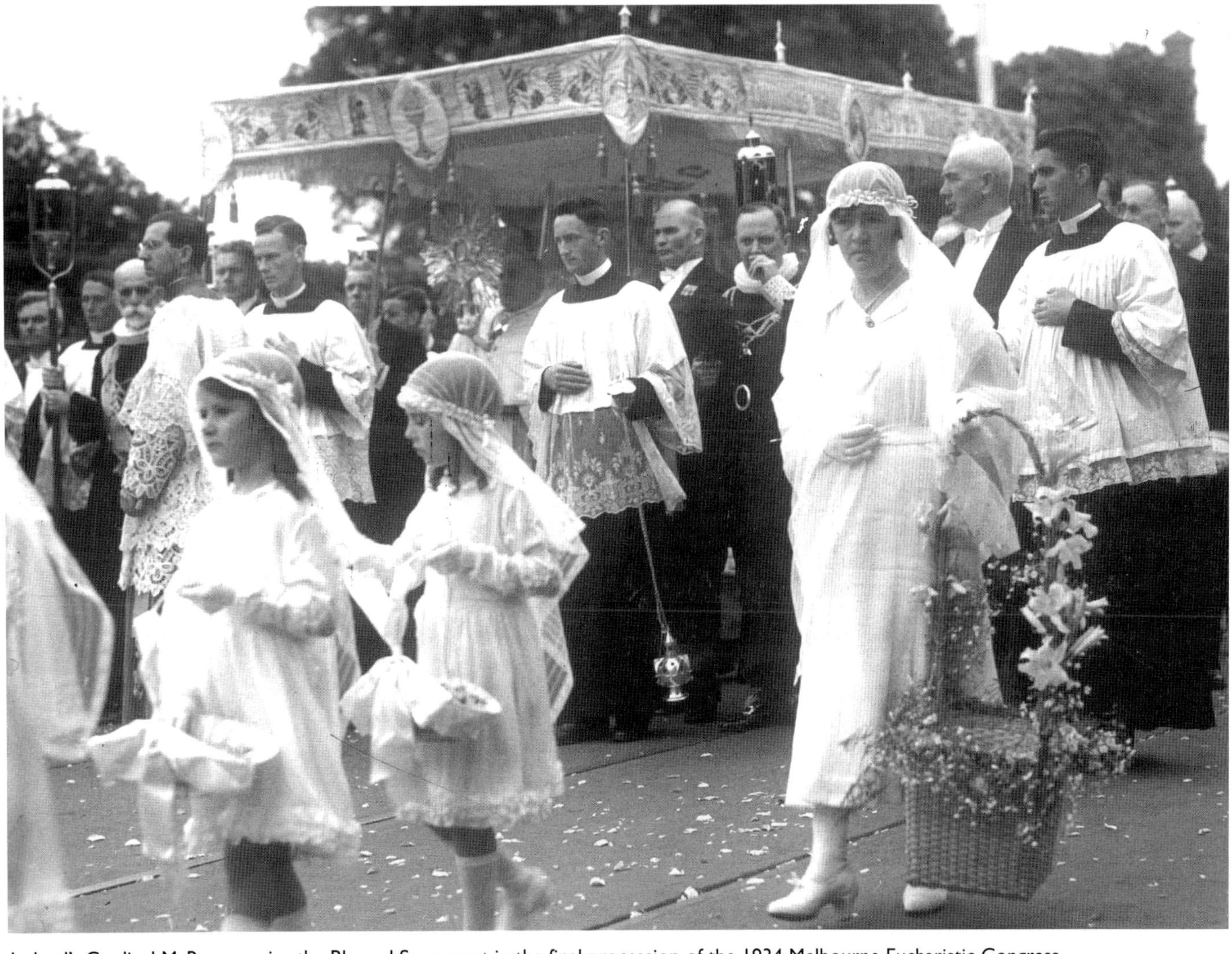

Ireland's Cardinal McRory carries the Blessed Sacrament in the final procession of the 1934 Melbourne Eucharistic Congress.

A note on the photographs:

In the interests of historical accuracy we would like to point out that the information given in this publication derives from newspaper cuttings and written captions attached to the original photographs. Whilst every effort has been made to ensure the accuracy of this information, we cannot be responsible for any inaccuracies that may have existed in the original text. If you are aware of any such errors, or can supply additional information about the photographs, we would very much like to hear from you at the address below.

Although the photographs are marked with exact dates, it is clear that in many instances these represented either the date that the picture was catalogued for publication, or the actual publication date, and not necessarily the precise day on which the event took place. Under the circumstances we have restricted the date to the year and month given, unless it has possible to confirm the exact day.

addenda:

From The Archives Volume one

Page 25 We identified a Fr. John Carwell SDB. His name was Fr. Eric Darwell.

From The Archives Volume Two

page 22 The Little Sisters of the Assumption were based in Wrexham at the time the picture was taken. The nun on the far left is Sr. Aidan.

From The Archives – Volume Three
produced in collaboration with The Universe Catholic weekly
1st Floor St. James's Buildings, Oxford Street, Manchester M1 6FP
Tel: 0161 236 8856 email: joseph.kelly@totalcatholic.com

Design and production: Joseph Kelly